DISCARD

28

Gifts of Writing

Gifts of Writing

Creative Projects with Words and Art

Susan and Stephen Judy

Charles Scribner's Sons
New York

Copyright © 1980 Stephen Judy and Susan Judy

Library of Congress Cataloging in Publication Data

Judy, Stephen N
Gifts of writing.

SUMMARY: Gives suggestions for combining creative
writing, calligraphy, and art work to produce unique
and personal gifts such as stationery, postcards,
posters, greeting cards, books of several types, and
holiday projects.
1. Handicraft—Juvenile literature.
2. Authorship—Juvenile literature. 3. Calligraphy—
Juvenile literature. 4. Books—Juvenile literature.
[1. Handicraft. 2. Creative writing. 3. Books.
4. Calligraphy] I. Judy, Susan J., joint author.
II. Title.
TT160.J83   745.594   80-10360
ISBN 0-684-16522-8

3 5 7 9 11 13 15 17 19 F/C 20 18 16 14 12 10 8 6 4 2

Printed in the United States of America

This book is a gift for our parents:

Jane and Woody Schmidt
Ann and Nelson Judy

Contents

viii

Introduction

The Joys of Writing and Giving

Few gifts are more satisfying to give or receive than writing. When you write, you put something of *yourself* on paper—*your* ideas, *your* imagination, *your* personality. Other people can learn about you through your writing, and you will probably enjoy getting to know others as they write for you.

The pleasure of giving is greater when the writing has been made attractive through artwork, and that's what this book is all about. We will describe a number of writing projects that we think you'll enjoy—from writing personalized greeting cards to making up your own detective thriller. Then we'll show you ways to make your project artistically interesting by doing things like creating illustrations, designing a book cover, or displaying your writing on a poster. We'll show you how to make a cloth binding for a book of your own, how to make a book that unfolds like an accordian, how to use your school photo in a Valentine's Day autograph album, and how to write on eggshells.

You can give writing to just about anyone at any time. You can write for special occasions or for no occasion at all. Some of the young people we know have prepared writing gifts for celebrations like birthdays or holidays. In addition, many of the projects we describe can be "given" in school, and the arts and crafts techniques that you learn from this book will help you brighten up the written assignments you give to your teacher.

If you ask at school, you can probably learn about writing contests and art fairs where you might be eligible to show your work and compete for prizes. While winning a writing contest or a youth talent fair award won't put any cash in your jeans, it can give you great personal pride and satisfaction, part of the joy of preparing gifts of writing.

Basic Tools, Materials, and Procedures

You don't need a lot of equipment to get started with a writing project. A sharp pencil or ball-point pen and a blank sheet of paper will usually get you going on the writing part. For the artwork, we will list the materials you need with each project. Most of these are available inexpensively, and you probably have many of them around the house. If you want to stock up beforehand, the basic materials which you'll use regularly include:

- Plain white paper
- Colored construction paper
- Scissors
- Paste or rubber cement
- Transparent tape
- Colored felt-tip markers, crayons, and/or pens
- Pencils—assorted colors
- Stiff cardboard or poster board
- Erasers
- Ruler

Other odds and ends that might come in handy include string, rubber bands, stapler, an Exacto knife or razor blade (use those only with permission), a paper punch, and scraps of yarn, ribbon, and cloth.

Some Pointers on Writing

Many writers like to seek out a "special" place to do their work. We

Bulletin board for notes and drafts

Book shelf mounted on wall for dictionary, favorite books, etc.

Pens and pencils (in tin can covered with construction paper)

Box for scraps, erasers, scissors, etc.

Ruler

Handy stack of writing paper

GLUE

Drawer for art supplies

Writer's Nook #1: A desk set up for writing and artwork.

Use clipboard or large piece of stiff cardboard for writing.

Writer's Nook #2: A comfy beanbag chair in the corner.

know one young person who likes to write up in the attic, even on summer days when the temperature soars to ninety. Another person always writes in a notebook while he lies belly down underneath the dining room table. A third claims she can only write inside her closet by the light of a flashlight, but we don't recommend that—it's too hard on the eyes. Look for a place that feels comfortable to you, a place that is a natural one for you to write when your inspiration is high. You might even want to set up your own "nook" or "cubby" like one of those shown in the drawing.

Plan to start writing what writers call a "rough" draft. Put down your ideas on scratch paper. (Don't use up your art materials right away.) With a rough draft you can change words you don't like, move sentences around, and try experimenting with the language you use. We like to read our rough drafts aloud to one another and ask for comments and suggestions. You might want to do the same, asking a brother or sister, a parent, or a friend to listen to what you have written. Then you can *revise* (change) your draft to make it say exactly what you want.

The final step before moving on to the artwork is to check your writing for spelling errors and the correct use of capitals, commas, and so on. Your parents or an older brother or sister can often help. You can use a dictionary to make certain everything is spelled correctly and to check the meaning of the words you use.

Then do the arts and crafts work following the instructions. If you are careful, we're certain your projects will turn out well. You'll be happy with both your writing and your artistry. However, as you do more and more projects, you'll have many ideas of your own, ideas for writing and ideas for new and different ways of doing the art. Feel free to follow your imagination and to invent your own projects.

Part One

Gifts-of-Writing Projects

Making Your Own Stationery

For letters that bear your own personal mark or touch, write on stationery that you have created. Or, make stationery as a gift for someone else, decorating the pages to reflect the personality of that person.

One-of-a-Kind Stationery

Materials:
- Paper—typing paper, blank letter-writing paper, textured paper, or other fancy paper from an art supply store
- Felt-tip pens, watercolors or poster paint, or crayons

Procedures:
If you are making one-of-a-kind stationery for yourself you can develop a new design for each new letter you write, depending on the mood you are in and the person you are writing to. You might decorate the pages of a letter to your grandma with flowers or drawings of your family. For a friend who is an animal lover, you can draw or paint horses, dogs, cats, or other animals on each sheet of paper. You might even try your hand drawing your own cartoon versions of Snoopy, Iggy, or Superman for your friends. You can write your initials in different ways, or you can make colorful shapes and designs rather than pictures.

Put your designs anywhere on the page—along the top, down the sides, along the bottom, in the corners, or in the center. You might even like to make a large design in very pale watercolors and to write *over* it once it dries.

Though you will probably want to decorate the stationery before you begin the letter, you can leave spaces as you write the letter and add pictures to illustrate the contents of the letter.

Stationery with Repeated Designs

You can decorate many sheets of paper quickly using simple print-making techniques.

Materials:
- Paper—different types: plain, colored, fancy
- Poster paint
- Small paint brushes

- Sharp knife or single-edged razor blade
- Cardboard
- Glue
- Potatoes or other fruits and vegetables: carrots, apples, etc.
- Small odds and ends—paper clips, coins, screws, washers, bottle caps, corks, spools, safety pins, matchsticks
- Old newspaper

Procedures:

To make prints for your stationery, begin by cutting a potato in half. Using the sharp point of a knife, cut the outline of a design into the meat of the potato. Now carve away all of the potato around the design, so that

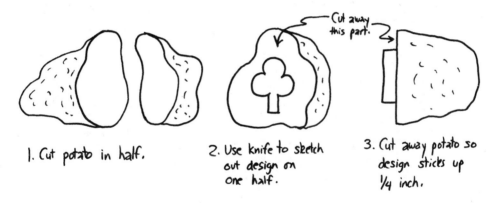

1. Cut potato in half.

2. Use knife to sketch out design on one half.

3. Cut away potato so design sticks up ¼ inch.

your design sticks up from the potato about ¼ inch.

Brush your design with poster paint and test the stamp by pressing it on a piece of newspaper. Adjust your design by carving away parts you don't want to show on the paper. After you have your design the way you want it, decorate your blank sheets by repeating the design along one side, the top, or the bottom of the page.

You can also carve away what is *inside* the outline rather than *outside* to make an interesting design. Experiment! Try cutting away more or less of the potato. Use an apple or a carrot instead of a potato.

Small objects can also be used to make designs on your stationery.

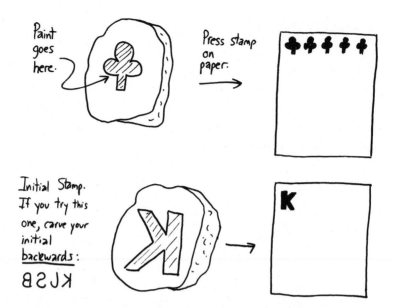

Paint goes here.

Press stamp on paper.

Initial Stamp. If you try this one, carve your initial backwards:

KJSB

Gather some nuts, bolts, screws, paper clips, coins, spools, etc., and experiment with designs. Brush the object with paint and press it on the

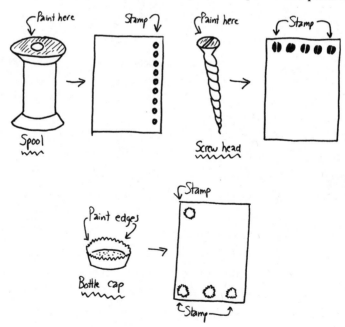

Paint here

Stamp

Spool

Paint here

Stamp

Screw head

Paint edges

Bottle cap

Stamp

Stamp

paper. Alternate objects to come up with a pattern you would like on your stationery.

Printed Stationery

To have stationery actually printed is more expensive than making your own, but it makes a perfect gift for someone special.

Materials:
- White paper—8½ x 11 inches
- Black pen, paint, or marking pencil
- Light blue pencil
- Transfer lettering (optional)

Procedures:
In order to have your stationery printed offset, you will need to make a black design on white paper. Anything black on the page will be printed, so be careful not to smudge or blot. Light blue pencil will not reproduce, so use that color for any preliminary sketches and to lay out rules or guidelines.

You may use any of the techniques described so far in making printed stationery—freehand or printed pictures and designs. You can also purchase transfer lettering and border designs to give your stationery a more professional (but less personal) look. Transfer lettering is available at art and school supply stores in a variety of styles and sizes. You may use it to put names or nicknames or addresses on the stationery.

Costs for offset printing vary from printer to printer and with the quality of paper and the color of ink you choose. One hundred copies of a single sheet on lightweight colored paper with black ink usually cost $5 to $7. Using heavier paper increases the price, and colored inks can be quite expensive. You can get many sheets of attractive personally designed stationery, however, at the minimal price.

You can make twice as much stationery for the same price with two different designs by using half sheets (4¼ x 5½ inches) rather than the full-size sheet. Simply divide the large sheet in half and make a different design for each half. When you take the sheet to the printer he will be able to cut the sheets in half for a slight additional fee.

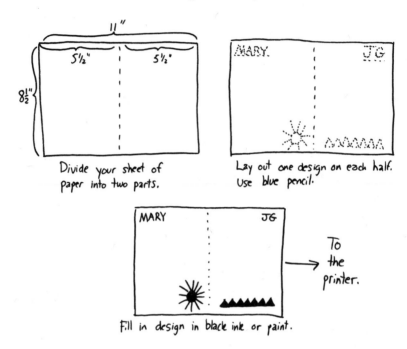

Divide your sheet of paper into two parts.

Lay out one design on each half. Use blue pencil.

Fill in design in black ink or paint.

To the printer.

Calligraphy and Penmanship

Throughout this book we will be suggesting ways to decorate your writing with color, designs, and illustrations. Another way to make your writing look as good as it reads is the printing or handwriting you use. You may have access to a typewriter for some of your writing projects. But you may need—or want—to do many of your projects in your own handwriting. The art of decorative penmanship is called "calligraphy."

The most important aspect of any project you create is legibility. You want people to be able to *read* what you have written. Some people feel that they can write more legibly in cursive or longhand. Other writers prefer to print. In making your final copy, use whatever form you feel you do best. You might try experimenting with your writing to see if you can make it more attractive or interesting.

Experimenting with Writing Tools

Materials:
- Pencils—#1 and #2 gray and in various colors
- Colored chalk
- Charcoal pencils
- Crayons
- Felt-tip pens—fine, medium, and broad widths
- Ball-point pens—fine, medium, wide points
- Fountain pens—varying width tips
- Scratch paper (different types)—bond, tissue, newspaper

Procedures:
Gather whatever writing implements you have available. Then try writing the same word with different tools and see how different the word can look. Also write the word in different sizes and colors.

Anger Anger Anger Anger Anger

Now write a whole poem or a saying, changing your writing tool to suit each word. Play with the size of the words, too.

Cherries Fresh from the Tree

Alphabets

Materials:
- Paper
- A variety of writing tools

Procedures:

Now that you have experimented with size and color and writing tools, try experimenting with the shape of your letters. Begin with tall, skinny writing. Make your vertical lines long and close together and your horizontal lines short. Make round letters into tall ovals.

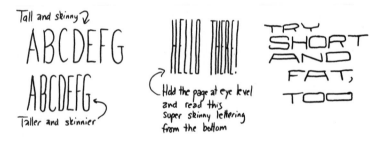

Now make block letters, making sure that none of your lines has curves and that every one of the letters is straight. Square off all points. Try some balloon writing next, keeping the letters fat and round.

Curlicue writing can be used for both cursive and printing. Put decorations and squiggles at the ends of words or letters.

After you have experimented with making letters in different shapes, try changing the slant of your letters. Write a whole story experimenting with sizes, shapes, colors, and slants of letters.

Postcards

If you like to save money (and who doesn't?), sending postcards instead of letters saves you over a nickel every time you write. And if you don't have a lot to say, postcards are perfect for delivering short messages. Although you can buy postcards—either plain or with photographs—sending one you made yourself will mean a great deal more to the person to whom you send it.

Materials:
Postcards are usually printed on something called "card" stock. The simplest thing to do is to buy some index cards, 4 x 6 inches. These cards also come in a variety of attractive colors, and they come with or without lines printed on one side. If you want to make a larger card, or, perhaps, one with an unusual shape, cut it out of heavy paper or a filing folder. *Caution:* If you make your card larger than 4 x 6 inches, if you make it in an unusual shape, or if it is made out of heavy material, you may have to pay letter-rate postage.

The Monogram Card

The simplest card is one with the address on one side and your message

11

on the other. On the message side, draw a monogram—your initials done in a fancy print style. You can also surround the edges of the card with a frilly border. You can draw monogram cards one at a time as you need them, or use any of the printing techniques that you learned in *Making Your Own Stationery.*

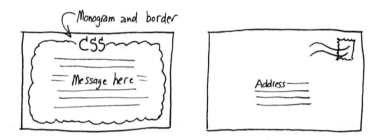

Picture Postcards

For this project, the message *and* the address go on one side of the card. (Put the message on the left side of the card, the address on the right.) The art takes up the whole other side.

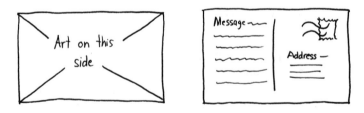

The art might be:
- A sketch or drawing done in pencil, pen, felt-tip marker, or crayon. (Be sure to use something that won't smudge or won't run if it gets wet.)
- Printed or stamped designs.

- A poem or short descriptive piece of writing with a design or illustration to accompany it.

Letter-Cards

If your message is long, or if you want it to be private so that no one else can read it, consider a letter-card. To make one, take *two* index cards and tape them together along the longer edge. Or, use a larger piece of card stock and fold it in half. Your message goes on the inside. When the card is folded, the address goes on one side and the artwork on the other. *Note:* You will need to use letter-rate postage with this card.

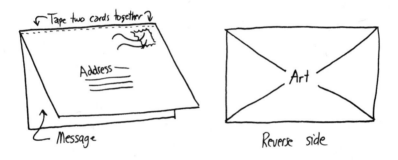

Antique Postcards

If you ever go to a garage sale or a flea market where old things are sold, look for antique postcards. You can buy them very inexpensively, and they're lots of fun to look at. You will probably find pictures of your town many years ago, scenic pictures from yesteryear, pictures of old cars, stores, and houses. Even though the pictures aren't your own, you might enjoy sending notes using these old cards. One writer we know actually made up stories to go with the old photographs on the front of the card. For example, if you found a card showing a 1922 beach scene, you might write a postcard-length story, "My Day at the Beach," imagining what it was like and telling a friend about it.

Continued-Story Postcards

Entertain a friend for several weeks or months. Send him or her a story in "installments," one chapter at a time, using postcards. You could fill one whole side of a card with this week's episode, or you could send a picture postcard with the story on half of one side and an appropriate illustration for the story on the other.

Posters

Posters reflect people's interests, personalities, and moods with pictures of famous people, scenery, sporting events, or animals, or with funny sayings, famous quotations, or poetry. You can make personalized posters for youself that express something important about you; you can make posters especially designed to fit friends and relatives; you can make posters to commemorate or celebrate special occasions.

Materials:
- Poster board or heavy paper—colored or white; at least 2 x 3 feet
- Rubber cement or glue
- Writing tool—crayon, felt-tip pen, paint and brush
- Pictures and photographs—from your own collection and/or from magazines
- Scissors

The Me Poster

The Me Poster should be a reflection of you—of what you want to tell the world about yourself. You can display photographs of important events in your life with captions or short stories about the pictures. You can include excerpts of stories or poems you have written. You might want to include some or all of the following: magazine pictures of your favorite hobbies, excerpts from favorite stories or books, song lyrics, sayings you have made up, poems you love, pictures of your best friend or members of your family with short descriptions or stories about them.

Gather all the materials you think you would like to include on your poster, but be prepared to discard items that don't seem to belong to your overall pattern. You may have collected so many things that they all won't fit.

Write out the captions, stories, and poems on separate pieces of paper to get an idea how much space they take up. When you have laid out your poster and you have all the pictures, photographs, sayings, and stories where you want them, glue everything down. You can also add border designs surrounding the entire poster or individual pictures or sayings. (See *Making Your Own Stationery* for ideas on printing techniques.)

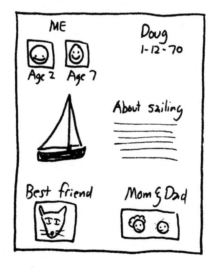

The Me Poster will be a nice gift to give to your parents, your grandparents, or your best friend. You might also want to make a poster for someone close, a poster about that person.

The Mood Poster

The basic procedures for the Mood Poster are the same as those for the Me Poster, but this one has a slot that allows you to change the poster so that each day it differs according to your moods.

Begin by designing a poster like the Me Poster, but this time cut two vertical slits. On each side of the poster board, measure 5 inches in from the edge; then draw a line 4½ inches long. Use a single-edged razor blade or scissors to cut this slit.

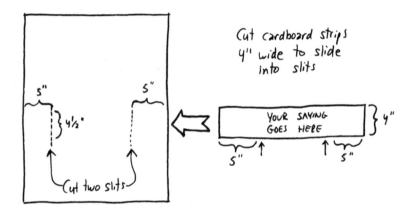

Use a second piece of poster board to make the strips to slide through the slits. Measure and cut a 2 x 3 foot poster board into nine 4-inch strips. Then write your poems and sayings on the strips. If you use both sides of each strip, you will have eighteen ways of expressing your ideas or moods for the day. Remember that you won't be able to write across the entire strip of poster board. When you slide the strip into your poster, draw a light line on each side to show where the strip is covered by the poster. Do your writing within those lines.

Here are some ideas for writing on your strips—some are things you can write yourself; some are things you can find that are already written:

- A verse from your favorite song—about friendship, dancing, loneliness, conflicts.
- A saying or poem about rain, sunshine, snow, cold; winter, summer, spring, fall.
- A saying or poem about flowers, cats and dogs, mountains, birds, horses, tigers, rivers, or lakes.
- A saying or poem about fighting, love, freedom, parents, peace, fear, winning, losing.
- A word or two—*Hurray! YUK! Stay Away! Genius Working, Cry Time, Please Knock, I'm Friendly, Hello Blues, Happy Holiday, Nap Time.*
- Pictures or symbols to accompany the writing.

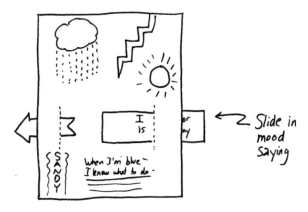

The Special Occasion Poster

Make a poster as part of your preparation for Halloween, Thanksgiving, Valentine's Day, Christmas, the birthdays of friends or family. Put your poster on a prominent door or wall, or perhaps on the front door of your house or apartment to share with neighbors or passersby.

Includes pictures, drawings, photographs, poems, stories, jokes, riddles, and designs appropriate to the occasion. See sections on *Greeting Cards* and *Holiday Projects* for more ideas.

Your Family Tree

All of us have our "roots," a string of ancestors whose blood is in our veins. Many people enjoy tracing their roots as a way of discovering just who they are. How much do you know about your ancestors? Who was your great-grandmother on your father's side? When was she born? Where did she live? Did you realize that about one-eighth of your physical characteristics are inherited from her? Wouldn't it be interesting to learn more about her and a dozen or two more of your relatives? Making a family tree is a project that takes some time and will probably involve quite a bit of letter writing. But the result is very satisfying, something that both you and other members of your family will enjoy studying and talking about in years to come.

Materials:
- Stationery and stamps
- Loose-leaf notebook
- Large cardboard or poster board
- Drawing pens or markers

Procedures:
The family tree begins with you and your brothers and sisters (if you have any) at the center, as the trunk. Then it branches upward and outward with your parents (two) and their parents (four people, your grandparents) and *their* parents (eight people, your great-grandparents). You can extend the tree almost indefinitely, and experts can trace a family ancestry back hundreds of years to thousands of people. But for a beginning, you might want to limit yourself to the main branches of your family as shown in the tree.

For each person on this tree, you will want to collect as much of the following information as possible:

- Date of birth
- Date of death (if the person has died)
- When and where married
- Names of children
- Places where he/she lived
- Education
- Jobs or occupations held
- Interesting stories about him/her

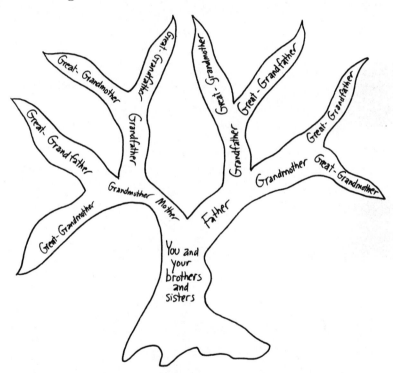

Keep all of this information in a loose-leaf notebook, allowing a page for each person. When you are finished with this project, you may also want to bind the pages of the notebook into a finished book. (See *A Hand-Bound Book*.)

Step 1. Interview one or both your parents to obtain as much information as you can about each of the people on the tree. You will also need to get addresses for people so that you can write letters to seek more information.

Step 2. When you have gotten all the information that you can from your parents, start writing to people like your grandparents. Explain what you are doing and the information that you are trying to get. You might even include a sheet of paper labeled with the name of each person you are inquiring about so that the person you are writing can simply fill in the blanks. Remember, because some of the people on the tree will probably have died, you will need to get reports on them from other people's memories. Paste all the letters you receive in your notebook as well, so that you will have a sample of the person's handwriting and his or her own story.

Step 3. On your large sheet of cardboard, draw the basic outline of the tree as shown in the diagram.

Step 4. As you collect information, write the basic facts about each person on the tree. You'll probably have to write small to squeeze in as much as possible. Another idea is to type the information on a small sheet of paper, then paste it to the tree.

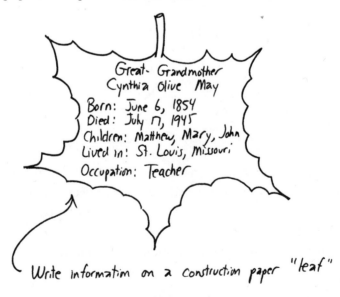

Great-Grandmother
Cynthia Olive May
Born: June 6, 1854
Died: July 17, 1945
Children: Matthew, Mary, John
Lived in: St. Louis, Missouri
Occupation: Teacher

Write information on a construction paper "leaf"

When you have collected as much information as you can, you might want to decorate the tree some more, to make it look as if it actually has leaves and branches. If you have photographs of people, you can add those to the tree as well. Finally, remember to save your notebook because of all the family facts it contains.

Follow-up:

You can extend your tree in many directions. For instance, you might want to try to learn something about your great-great-grandparents, who probably lived two hundred years ago, possibly on another continent like Europe or Africa. Or, you might trace your grandparents' other children (your aunts and uncles) and *their* children (your cousins). See how far you can extend the branches of your family tree.

Greeting Cards

Greeting cards abound. People send greeting cards for birthdays, anniversaries, graduation, Halloween, Christmas, Chanukah, Easter, Passover, Valentine's Day, Father's Day, Mother's Day; they send thank you cards, sympathy cards, get well cards, have-a-nice-trip cards, why-haven't-you-written cards, enjoy-your-new-home cards, hello-how-are-you cards, I-like-you cards, and cards for no reason at all. Not only can you save a lot of money by making your own cards, you can also show special caring by creating a card suited to the person receiving it.

Materials:
- Paper—heavy paper works best
- Pencils, pens, markers, paint
- Scissors (and pinking shears, if you have them)
- Glue

- Odds and ends from around the house—aluminum foil, yarn or ribbon, fabric scraps, beads, old cards, nature materials (leaves, dried flowers, etc.)

Procedures:

In making your own greeting cards, you can use a great variety of materials. Use fabric to give your greeting cards texture. Dress characters you draw on your card in bits of fabric cut in the shape of pants, shirts, dresses. Use felt or fuzzy material on the animal shapes you draw. Cut hearts, fruit, flowers, and trees out of brightly colored felt, satin, velvet, or knit scraps. Use beads and buttons to decorate the designs you draw. And, after writing your words, glue yarn or felt strips over them to make the lettering.

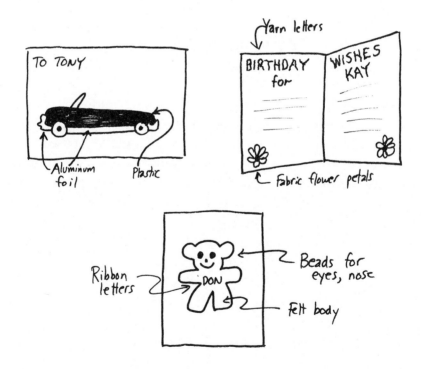

Use different sizes for the greeting cards you make, too. Make an oversized card using two 8½ x 11 inch sheets that you glue at the side or sew together with yarn. You can make four mini-cards by cutting an 8½ x 11 inch sheet into four pieces. Make mini-mini-cards by folding each of *those* pieces twice, or, if you have very heavy paper, cutting each of those pieces in half again. (However, the envelope you use to mail your cards must be at least 3½ x 5 inches to follow postal regulations.)

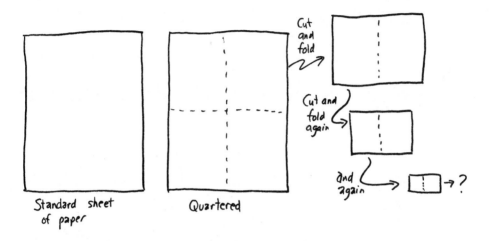

Standard sheet of paper   Quartered

To make shaped cards, fold your paper in half. Draw your design with the fold line as one edge of your design. When you cut out the design, leave the fold line uncut.

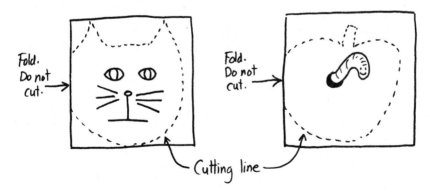

Use windows in your cards for special effects. Fold your paper in half. On the second page draw or write the picture or words that you want to reveal through your window. Hold the folded card up to the light and, on the front page, draw lightly with pencil around the section you want to be the window. If your paper is too thick to see through, measure from the top, bottom, and sides of your picture on page two and then measure those distances onto page one. Cut the window to reveal the picture on the second page.

Draw art on page two

Trace outline for window on page one.

Cut out window so art shows through.

You also might want to try different ways of folding your greeting cards. (*Part II: Making Your Own Books* contains sections on *Scrolls; Accordian Books;* and *Quartos* that can give you ideas.)

Birthday Cards

The best thing about making your own cards is that you can personalize the message. What you write on the card is especially designed for the person receiving the card. Think about using some of the following in your message:

- A list of wishes. What does the person like the most? Tennis? Horses? Bicycles? Hot fudge sundaes? Insects? Summer? Swimming? Snow? Skiing? Make a list of wishes and include the person's favorites.

- A list of promises or gifts of yourself. Give your mother the gift of babysitting for your little sister a couple of afternoons; promise your dad a wash or wax for his car; promise your parents a month of keeping your room clean without their asking you to do it; promise your grandmother a letter every month for a year; give your best friend a month of helping with his/her housework or yardwork; give your little brother five nights of help with his homework.

- A story—fact or fiction—about the person to whom you are giving the card. Write your version of a special event (a trip to Florida, last year's birthday, a sports victory, a ballet recital). Or, make up a wonderful fantasy about the person.

- A list of memoirs. Start the list with "I remember" or "Remember when" and then write out your memories of all the special or interesting things that have happened to the birthday person since his or her last birthday.

- Jokes and riddles. Some people like elephant jokes, some like "knock-knock" jokes, and some like riddles and rhymes. Find some new jokes and riddles to add to your friend's collection. (Note: Cards with folding doors are a good idea for riddles and jokes. Put the riddle or the first part of the joke on the outside of the door. The person opens the door to find the answer or punch line.)

Get Well Cards

Though any of the ideas for birthday cards would work fine for get well cards, it's also nice to give someone sick at home or stuck in bed something to do. Make activities on large cards (8½ x 11 inches) or on cards that are booklets (three or four 8½ x 11 inch sheets folded in half and stapled or tied with yarn). Use one or several of the following activities:

25

Maze. Mazes can be made of varying difficulty depending on the age of the person who is to do it. After making a sample maze, you might want to try it out on someone the same age as the recipient to see if it's the right degree of difficulty. To make sure it works start by making the correct path, then add dead end paths to complicate it.

Word Search. Create a theme for your word search based on the person's interests; then make a list of the words you are going to use. Hide the words in a block of letters either across or down. Begin by making your words and then fill in the extra letters. Graph paper can be helpful in making your letters evenly spaced.

Write in the
words.

Then hide them in
other letters.

Dot-to-Dot. Begin by drawing a picture on a piece of scratch paper the size you want your final puzzle to be. Go over your drawing in dark felt-tip or ink pen. Place your actual card over your drawing and trace the picture by making dots at intervals around the outside of your drawing. (You may have to hold the drawing and your card up to the light to do this.) Remember that the person doing the dot-to-dot will make straight lines between dots, so make sure that dots are close together where there is a curve. After you have completed making the dots, number them consecutively around the outside of the drawing, remembering that the person doing the dot-to-dot will not lift his/her pencil.

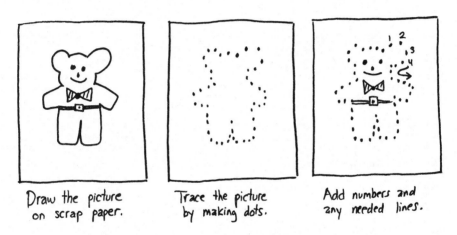

Draw the picture on scrap paper.   Trace the picture by making dots.   Add numbers and any needed lines.

Which One Is Different? Make several drawings—four or five—all identical in every way, then make one slightly different. The person who gets the card has to figure out which one is different.

27

Secret-Friend or Admirer Cards

If you want to baffle a friend, or if you like someone but you don't want to tell him or her outright, send anonymous cards you have made yourself. You could make up riddles that hint at your identity but don't give it away. Or you might want to tell stories about yourself or about the other person and let him or her try to discover your identity through the hints they receive in those. Deliver cards through a mutual friend sworn to secrecy, or slip them into the person's desk, coat pocket, or locker. Secret-friend cards are guaranteed to get you through a cold and boring winter.

Cards for No Reason at All

It's always a treat to look forward to receiving cards on special occasions, but it's also great to receive a card unexpectedly. Design some "no-reason-at-all" cards to send to faraway relatives or friends, or spend a day making "Happy Sunday" or "Have a Good Week" cards for your parents, your teachers, your best friends.

Memoirs

Many people save treasures—remembrances of special occasions in their lives. Some save photographs. Some buy postcards or T-shirts or knickknacks to remind them of special places they have visited. Some save programs from plays or concerts or sporting events to remember the occasion. People save old letters, greeting cards, and even ribbons from packages as mementos.

A written account of an occasion—a memoir—can be an even more valuable remembrance, because it reflects your unique reaction, your special feelings about something important in your life.

You can also write memoirs to keep or to share with another person. You may want to write about an event shortly after it occurs and give it to the person right away. Or you may want to write something to give to a person some time later. You may even want to write about something that happened a long, long time ago that made an impression on you.

Here are some memoirs you might like to write:

- For your grandparents, describing the festivities of a wedding anniversary party.
- For your little brother or sister, describing the day he or she was born and how you felt on that day.
- For your parents, describing your feelings about a birthday party or a special gift they gave you.
- For a camp counselor, describing the camp experience that you liked best or the funniest or scariest event at camp.
- For your best friend, describing the day he/she won the track or swim meet or pitched an outstanding game.
- For your family, about Christmas or another holiday.
- For your teacher, about an enjoyable day of school.
- For a friend, about a place that made a special impression on you both.
- For your friend, about important experiences you have shared: camp, birthday parties, cookouts, sleep-overs, school activities.

After you have written your memoir, think of how to present it. You might like to use photographs you have taken, or you can draw pictures to illustrate your memoir. (See *Calligraphy and Penmanship* for some ideas on how to make your handwriting decorative. Several sections in Part II, *Making Your Own Books*, will give you ideas for making a memoir, or a collection of several, into a book.)

Fortune Cookies

You may have eaten fortune cookies for dessert at a Chinese restaurant. They are crisp, sweet cookies, hollow inside, that contain a brief message or fortune. Chinese cookie fortunes are generally pretty serious, telling you about business dealings or your health. We suggest making up some wacky fortunes, then inserting them in your own, home-baked cookies to give to friends.

Materials (for the fortunes):
- Paper
- Pens or typewriter
- Scissors

Procedures:
Cut about twenty-five thin strips of paper, about ¼ inch wide and 2½ inches long.

On each strip write a funny fortune. (Note: If you use a typewriter, type the fortunes on one big sheet of paper, then cut it into strips.) You'll have to write small. Keep your fortunes brief. Here are some that our kids wrote:

> Tomorrow your cat will smile.
> Watch for falling lightbulbs.
> You will spill ketchup soon.

Next, make the cookies.

Materials:
- 2 eggs
- 2/3 cup honey
- ½ cup butter or margarine

- 1¾ cups all-purpose flour
- 1 teaspoon almond or vanilla flavoring

Procedures:

1. Beat the two eggs in a bowl.
2. Slowly beat in 2/3 cup of honey.
3. Melt and then slowly add in ½ cup of butter or margarine.
4. Gradually blend in 1¾ cups flour.
5. Stir in almond or vanilla flavoring.
6. Beat the mixture until you have a smooth batter.

Heat a frying pan (Teflon or any no-stick pan if you've got one) on low heat. When it is hot, spoon on one tablespoon of batter and spread it with the back of the spoon into a circle about four inches across. Spread the batter just as thin as you can. You'll have to experiment a bit at this stage. If your batter is spread too thin, it will stick to the pan. If you don't get it thin enough, your cookies will turn out like pancakes and be soggy. Cook for about a minute and a half, till the underside is a medium brown. Then flip onto the other side and brown.

Remove the cookie from the pan and put it on a plate with the second side (the lighter-colored side) up. Take one of your fortune strips and place it in the center of the cookie.

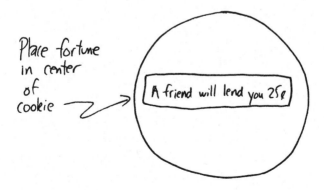

Place fortune in center of cookie ⟶

A friend will lend you 25¢

Fold the cookie in half, so that the fortune is enclosed in a half circle.

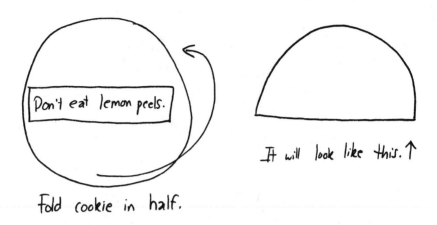

Don't eat lemon peels.

Fold cookie in half.

It will look like this. ↑

Now, with your thumbs, lift up the center of the folded side about half an inch, while drawing the edges around into a three-quarters circle with your fingers. This will create the twist that makes yours look like a real fortune cookie.

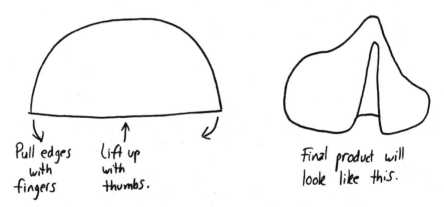

Pull edges with fingers

Lift up with thumbs.

Final product will look like this.

When you have made all your cookies, place them on an ungreased cookie sheet and bake them in the oven about ten minutes at 400 degrees. This will crisp up the cookies and make them toasty brown.

Share with friends and enjoy watching them read their fortunes.

May all your bad fortune cookies be eaten by mice (or your enemies)!

Part Two

Making Your Own Books

Scrolls

We all know about scrolls. Most of us envision the king's courtier as he unrolls and reads a royal document, proclaiming some special news. But scrolls can also make unusual books. They can be tucked into your pencil holder or propped up on a corner of your desk or dresser.

You can make your scroll almost any size, from a tiny one, just a few inches long, to a long one, many feet in length.

To make a simple scroll, take an 8½ x 11 inch sheet of paper, fold it in half the long way and cut it along the fold line. You can use one of these halves to make a scroll, or you can tape the two halves together, end to end.

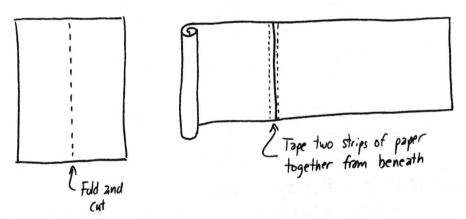

Fold and cut

Tape two strips of paper together from beneath

If you taped the halves together, now you have a long strip of paper 4¼ x 22 inches. You may add more strips to this scroll so a story of any length will fit on it. Of course, you can make your scrolls any width you wish by cutting the paper to size and by taping sections together.

You can also look around in stores for paper that comes in rolls. For narrow scrolls you can use adding machine or cash register tape. For wide scrolls, there is shelf paper, white or printed with colors and designs.

After you have written and illustrated your scroll, roll it up and deliver it. To roll your scroll, begin at the bottom and roll to the top with your story inside. Often it helps to roll it around something like a pencil or a cardboard tube that you remove later. To keep your scroll from unrolling, you will need some way to fasten it. Depending on the size you can:

- Put a rubber band around it.
- Tie it with a ribbon or piece of yarn.
- Decorate an empty toilet paper roll or paper towel roll and slide the scroll inside.
- Use an old napkin ring.
- Use an inexpensive finger ring from a gum machine or from the dime store.

A Scroll on Rollers

Materials:
- Round "rollers"—two dowel rods, cardboard tubes, or pencils
- A paper scroll
- Glue

Procedures:
Cut the rollers approximately four to six inches longer than the width of your scroll. Leave at least two inches of blank paper at the beginning and the end of your story. (You may need to leave a bit more if you use very large sticks.) Lay the scroll flat and place a stick at the top. The stick should be centered with an extension on each side of your paper. Apply

glue to the entire surface of the stick, except the two extensions. Roll the paper around the stick. Do the same at the bottom of the scroll.

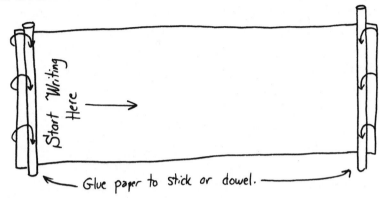

Allow your scroll to dry. If the scroll is not longer than arm's length, you can roll it up from the bottom and down from the top and make the two sticks meet in the middle. If it is a longer scroll, roll the paper onto the bottom stick. As you read, you will roll the paper onto the top stick.

The Box Scroll

For avid TV viewers, we present the box scroll or TV scroll. With this somewhat more elaborate scroll, your story and pictures pass through a viewers' screen made from a cardboard box.

Materials:
- Cardboard box—find a carton approximately 12 x 20 x 12 inches or larger
- Dowel rods—two rods, approximately five inches longer than the height of your box
- Shelf paper or paper taped in a long strip
- Poster paint or wrapping paper
- Felt-tip pens or crayons
- Scissors or single-edged razor blade
- Transparent or package sealing tape

Procedures:

Begin by making your TV "screen." First tape all the flaps of the box closed. On a large side of the box, draw the dimensions of your screen. The *height* of the screen should be slightly smaller than the width of the paper you will be using. Thus if your paper is twelve inches wide, you should make your screen ten inches tall. You can make your screen any width. Then cut out the screen.

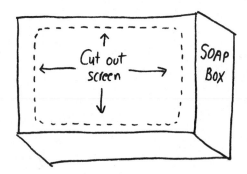

Now it's time to make your scroll. This time, instead of writing from top to bottom, you will create your story from left to right. You will also want to make your story in panels the width of your screen. Leave several inches of paper before the first panel to attach to the rod. Next, measure off an area the width of your screen for the title panel. Continue to measure off the same width for each panel in your story. Leave enough blank paper at the end for the area behind the screen and for fastening the scroll to the other dowel rod.

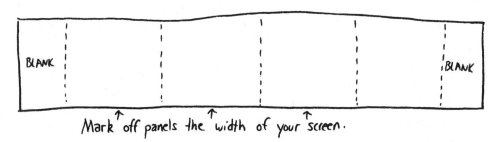

Mark off panels the width of your screen.

Decorate your box with poster paints or gift wrap. On either side of the screen make holes at the top and bottom of the box slightly larger than the rollers, which are about five inches longer than the height of your box. Push a rod through each hole at the top and into the hole at the bottom. Then fasten the scroll to the rods. Tape the end of the story to the dowel rod and roll the paper onto the rod with the pictures and story facing the screen. When you have reached the beginning of the story, stretch the paper across the screen and tape the beginning of the story to the other rod. You are now ready to show your TV story. Turn the rod you have just taped, rolling your story onto it so the viewer can watch your scroll.

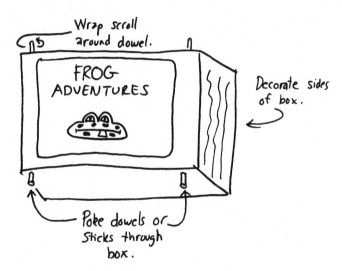

If you use tape to attach your scroll, you will be able to remove it and create several made-for-TV scrolls.

Here are some stories you can tell in a scroll:

Mystery Stories. The solution to the crime is hidden at the end of the scroll and it's impossible to sneak a peek without unrolling the whole scroll.

Picture Stories. Cut photographs and drawings from magazines and newspapers. Use rubber cement to glue them to the scroll (either a roller scroll or a box scroll). Then write stories and captions to accompany each picture.

Royal Tales and Proclamations. "Hear Ye, Hear Ye," says the courtier, reading the king's proclamation from a scroll. Make up some proclamations of your own, or write some fairy tales about the proclamations of a king or queen and what happens in the kingdom as a result.

Accordian Books

Accordian books, like the musical squeeze box, get longer and longer. Instead of turning pages, the reader unfolds them, one at a time. Depending on how long your story is, an accordian book may stretch out five feet or more. It makes an especially attractive display on a shelf, fireplace mantel, or bulletin board.

Materials:

- Sheets of cardboard or paper to make pages. Use stiff cardboard, poster board, heavy plain paper, or construction paper.
- Tape—either clear tape or colored cloth or plastic tape.
- Scissors.

Procedures:

Cut enough pages for the book. Lay out all the pages, side by side, on a flat surface like the kitchen floor. The pages can be placed the wide way or the tall way.

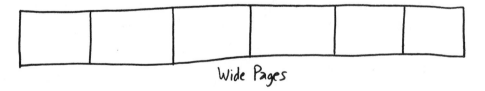

Wide Pages

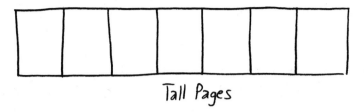

Tall Pages

Run a piece of tape down the seam between each page. If you use colored tape, choose a color that makes an attractive contrast to the color of your pages.

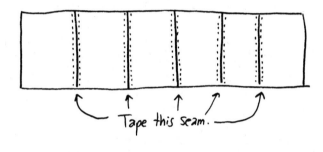

Tape this seam.

Carefully flip all the pages over and tape the seam on the back. Fold the book up (like an accordian) and you are ready to copy in your story.

COVER

Except for the cover, write on only one side of each sheet of paper, the side that faces you when you unfold the "accordian."

Here are some writing ideas that work well with accordian books:

Cartoon Story. On each page of your book draw pictures of your characters. Use balloons for the words that the characters speak, just like in the newspapers.

"And Then" Story. On page one of your book begin a tale with the usual opening, "Once upon a time." Each following page begins with the phrase, "And *then* . . ." As the story grows, make each "and then" bigger and wilder so that the story becomes more and more complicated and fantastic. When you reach the last page of your book, begin with the word "Finally . . ." and bring your story to an end.

Add-a-Character Story. Begin by describing a single character: a boy, a girl, an animal, a superhero. On each succeeding page add one new character, a person or animal who joins in the story. Soon you'll have a mob of characters on every page. Then, if you want, subtract-a-character for the rest of the book, taking away one character each page until you're left with the one you began with.

Photo Album. Make an accordian book with photos and captions on each page showing you at a different age (one, two, three, and so on). You can also show family holidays, vacations, or special events through the years. Or come up with your own idea for an accordian photo album.

Quartos

Quartos are books made by folding a piece of paper several times. Take a sheet of notebook paper or scrap paper and try some experimental folds. If you simply fold it in half, you create a leaflet with four pages. If you fold it again, you create eight pages. A third fold will create sixteen. The more you fold, the more pages you will have. Thus in making a quarto, you can create a book of many pages from a single sheet of paper.

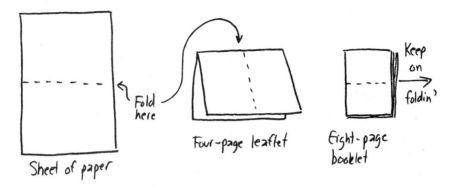

Sheet of paper

Fold here

Four-page leaflet

Eight-page booklet

Keep on foldin'

The larger the paper you start with, the bigger—in both length and size—your book can be.

An Unfolding Book

You may have received a birthday or holiday card that unfolds. It starts out regular size, but instead of turning its pages, you unfold the card so that it gets bigger and bigger as it goes along.

Materials:
- A sheet of paper—the larger the better. Use regular or oversize construction paper or even a large sheet of shelf paper.
- Drawing pens, pencils, or crayons.

Procedures:
First, fold your paper several times, three, four, or five times. Next, slowly unfold your book, writing a small page number on each page. The outside page will be #1. When you open it up, you have pages #2 and #3. Unfold it again and you get #4, etc.

Remember, the final number of pages in the book will be determined by the number of times you folded in the first place.

When you have finished unfolding and numbering, you will know how many pages you have in your book. Now refold the book and start telling your story.

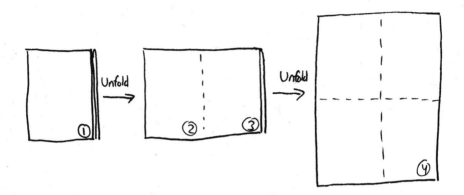

The stories that work best with an unfolding book are ones that get bigger and bigger or end with a surprise. For example, you might write an *Add-a-Character* story as described under *Accordian Books*. Or you might create a story where something explodes at the end, filling the final page with a drawing of clouds of smoke. One young person we know wrote and illustrated an unfolding book about how the sun grew from being a tiny little spark to a giant ball of fire. Another told a story of a dog that ate and ate and ate, until, on the very last page of the book, it turned into a pig. Once you have folded your paper and numbered the pages, an idea for a story may hit you.

Signature Book

In the publishing industry, "signature" is a term for a number of pages that are bound together. You can make a signature very easily through folding. Then you can turn it into a book.

Materials:
- Sheet of paper—the larger the better
- Stapler or needle and thread
- Scissors

Procedures:

Fold your paper as you did for the unfolding book—three, four, five, or more times—until you have a book about the size you want. Then staple or sew along the one edge that has only a single fold showing. This will bind all of the pages in your book together. Finally, use your scissors to trim around the remaining three edges. (*Don't* cut the edge where you have stitched or stapled.)

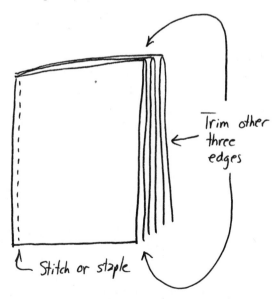

Trim other three edges

Stitch or staple

This kind of book can be used for just about any of the writing projects we have outlined. The outside pages serve as the cover; the inside will be for the story and artwork.

Fancy Folds

We often think of books as being square or rectangular, but there is no reason why they have to be. If you take a square sheet of paper and fold it in half one, two, or more times, you create a triangular book. What kind of story could you write to fit that triangle? With some scrap sheets, try a variety of different folds. See what kinds of patterns you can create. If you know a little origami, which is the Japanese art of making sculpture out of paper, you might use an origami sculpture for a book! Or why not write a story about flying on the wings of your very own flying paper-airplane book?

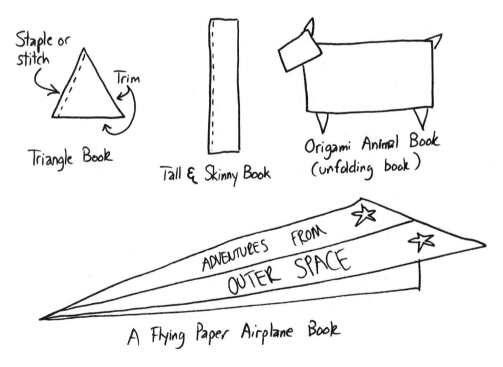

Staple or stitch

Trim

Triangle Book

Tall & Skinny Book

Origami Animal Book (unfolding book)

ADVENTURES FROM OUTER SPACE

A Flying Paper Airplane Book

Mini-Books

Mini-books come in many sizes—all of them small. A single 8½ x 11 inch sheet of paper can make a small eight-page book, a tiny sixteen-page book, or a microscopic thirty-two-page book.

Mini-books can be made like Quartos. Fold a sheet of paper in half several times. To keep the book together, open to the last fold and staple along the fold ½ inch from the top and ½ inch from the bottom. Then cut around the other three sides, so that the pages are all separated from one another.

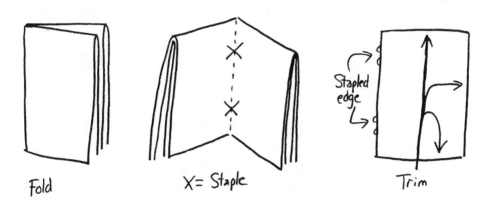

Fold   X = Staple   Trim

In order to make your story come out the right number of pages, you will need to plan in advance what will go on each page. Remember the size of your pages. You will not be able to get very many words or very elaborate pictures on the littlest books.

Very simple stories work best with mini-books. A series of mini-books that tell a continuing story is also fun to do. (Or you might want to write several different adventure books about the same character or group of characters that you tell about in a mini-book series.) Stories about little characters who live in little worlds and have little secrets and little adventures with little villains are fun to write about for your little books.

The Animated Mini-Book

The animated mini-book works best in the thirty-two-page size. In this book the characters seem to move as you flip the pages of the book quickly with your thumb. After you have made your book, make sure that your pages are trimmed very evenly. Then, decide what sort of action you want to take place in your book. Keep the movement very simple: a bunny hopping; a ball bouncing up and down; the sun rising over a mountain; a car moving along the road.

Your first picture goes on the very last page of your book. On the next to the last page, draw the same picture, changing the position of the figure only slightly. Continue to draw the figure on each page (front side only), each time changing the position of the figure slightly, until, by the time you have gotten to page thirty-two, you have completed the action.

You can now turn the book over and make another animated picture using the backs of the pages.

Show motion on individual pages.

Flip through pages rapidly to see action.

A Hand-Bound Book

Most of the books we have shown you so far have paper covers. In this project, we'll show you how to make one of the most satisfying of the writing activities: making a true bound book, with a cloth (or other kind) of cover. Because it takes a while to bind a book, this is the kind of gift you might want to reserve for someone special. It's also a place for you to put the very best of your writing.

Materials:
- Sheets of paper for pages
- Plain stiff cardboard
- Scissors
- White glue or contact cement (Look for contact cement at a hardware or drugstore. It is especially useful for this project.)
- Stapler or needle and thread
- Material for cover—a piece more than twice the size of your book. You may choose one of the following:
  Cloth (Look for a cloth "remnant" at a fabric store)
  Contact paper (This is plastic with adhesive on the back)
  Heavy wallpaper (Go to a paint or wallpaper store and ask for scraps. Try to get the kind that already has glue on the back.)
- Cloth tape or adhesive tape
- Ruler

Procedures:
1. After you have completed writing and illustrating your book, add one blank page at the front and back of the book. Then staple or sew the pages together about ¼ inch in from the left side.

Ⓐ Stack your pages with a blank sheet in front and one at the back

Blank

Blank

Ⓑ Then sew or staple the pages together.

2. Cut two pieces of stiff cardboard approximately ½ inch larger than your book.

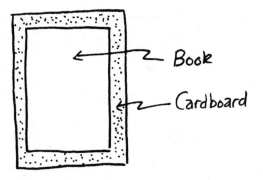

← Book

← Cardboard

3. Tape the two cardboard covers together, leaving about ½ inch between them. (If your book is especially thick, make the gap between cardboards as wide as the book is thick.)

TAPE

TAPE

Flip covers over so when you're through, tape is on back.

4. Cut a piece of cloth, wallpaper, or contact paper approximately ¾ inch larger than your taped-together cardboards. (If you are using contact, *do not* peel off the brown paper that protects the glue just yet.)

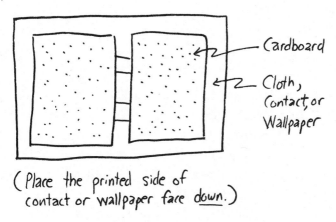

(Place the printed side of contact or wallpaper face down.)

5. Now fold over the edges and glue the cover material to the cardboard as shown on page 52. Start by turning down the "ears" of the corners. Then fold over the rest of the edge.

For cloth: Use white glue or contact cement. Be careful with white glue, because it may soak through the fabric and leave a mess if you use too much. With contact cement, put glue on the cloth and on the cardboard, wait ten minutes, and then press the two together. Be careful here, too, because the contact cement will stick together everything it touches.

For contact paper: Carefully peel off the protective brown paper. Do it slowly or the stuff will curl up and wrinkle or ruin the contact. Then center the cardboards in the air over the sticky side, and when everything looks right, gently press the book cardboards to the contact.

For wallpaper: If the paper does not have glue on the back, use white glue or contact cement as described for cloth. If it is preglued, moisten the glue side with a sponge and proceed as you would with contact paper.

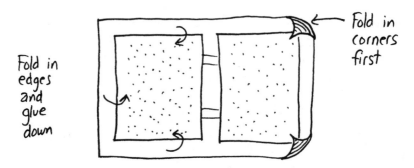

Fold in corners first

Fold in edges and glue down

6. Center the book pages over the cardboard/cloth covers. Glue the blank page at the front of your book to the cardboard on the left side and glue the blank page at the back to the right side cardboard. Carefully wipe up any spilled or oozed glue, and your book is finished. To press it perfectly flat, place it under a stack of heavy books for several hours.

Blank Page

TITLE PAGE by

Glue to cover

Card with title

TITLE

The Final Product

A hand-bound book can be used with a great many of the projects described in this book: *Stories and Mini-Novels; Family Stories; Original Holiday Tales; Books for Children;* or *A Spring Nature Journal.*

Note: Many young people we know like to make several copies of the same book, one to keep, others to give away. You might consider making photocopies of your pages, then setting up a kind of assembly line to make several covers at a time.

Books for Children

Is there a special child in your life? A brother or sister? A cousin or neighborhood kid? Maybe you babysit for some little children you especially like. The next time you would like to give them a gift, make it a book that you have written especially for them.

Children love to hear things about themselves. They constantly ask about the things they did when they were "little." Sometimes parents tell bedtime stories in which the child is the hero or heroine of the story. Write a story for children that is all about them. The story may be factual (one in which everything is true), describing an event or experience the children had when they were smaller. Or the story may be fiction (an adventure or fantasy that you make up) in which the children are the heroes. The story might tell about the children's . . .

- visit to Ice Cream Island.
- adventure on the starship *Enterprise*.
- day as King or Queen of Disneyland.
- first trip to Mars.
- discovery of a cave full of treasures.
- adventure with the escaped circus lion.
- day as the boss of the household.
- trip with Santa Claus to help deliver toys.
- life as a horse trainer or famous jockey.

In creating your fantasies or adventures, think about the things that really excite children. Then let your imagination go wild. Create wonderful sights. Describe impossible feats and accomplishments.

The child does not have to be a character in the book you write. You might like to base a book on some special interest the child has. Or you might know some books that the child especially likes that could give you some ideas about new books. What amuses the child? Does he or she like nonsense books? Riddle books? Does the child enjoy scary stories about ghosts and witches? (Some children are unusually frightened by that kind of story and have nightmares. Others relish spooky tales.) Is the child crazy about animals—dogs, horses, cats, any old animal? Does the child live in the city or the country? Would he or she be interested in tales of other places? Does the child like to swim? Go to the zoo? Ride amusement park rides? Go to school? Is there something the child is interested in learning now that you might use in a book? The alphabet? Numbers? The names of flowers or birds or different kinds of animals? Knowing the child, you can come up with lots of ideas for stories that you know would be enjoyable.

Another kind of story that children's authors write helps a child deal with some new or difficult experience. For example, some children are afraid of the dark. Some are picked on by big kids. Some children have trouble appreciating a new baby brother or sister and wish they were still the youngest and had all their parents' attention. Some children are apprehensive about starting kindergarten. Some children hate vegetables. Some are afraid of dogs. Some are afraid of water. Often it helps a child see other children—even children in books—dealing with the same problems. So, write a book for your favorite child in which a character solves that problem or learns a lesson. The book can be serious or funny, but be careful not to be "preachy" or to scare the child. Even though you might be discussing a problem in the book, your object should still be to entertain the child, to help him or her feel good personally and about the world.

Several projects in this book—*Scrolls; Accordian Books; Quartos; Mini-Books;* and *A Hand-Bound Book*—describe different types and sizes of handmade books. You might also consider using books of different shapes. Use the shape of a cat's head for a book about kittens, a witch outline for a scary story, a school building for a story about starting kindergarten.

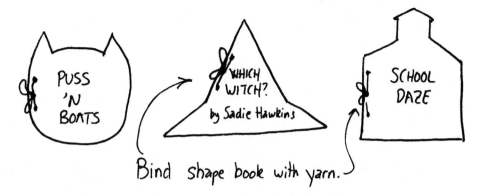

PUSS 'N BOATS

WHICH WITCH?
by Sadie Hawkins

SCHOOL DAZE

Bind shape book with yarn.

The simplest shape books can be made by making a large cover in a special shape and leaving pages rectangular. But you can also use the cover as a stencil to cut pages in the same shape as the cover. Use yarn or ribbon to bind one side of your book.

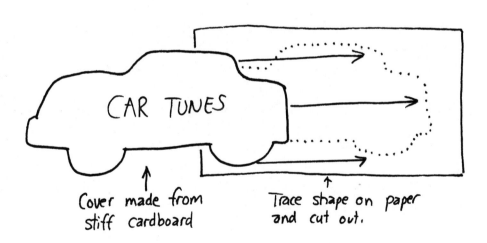

CAR TUNES

Cover made from stiff cardboard

Trace shape on paper and cut out.

Collaborative Books

Collaborative books are made with someone else. There are a variety of ways of sharing the task of writing a book, and you and your partner can work out an arrangement that makes the best use of your writing and artistic talents. One way of collaborating is to have one person do the writing while the other person does the illustrations.

In creating your book, either the pictures or the story may come first. Perhaps you have a friend who is good at drawing superheroes or animals. His or her pictures might be the starting point for a story you write. The two of you can get together to talk about how the pictures and the story can be combined. Or you might have a terrific idea for a story and you know someone who could make pictures to accompany your writing. Collaborate on the development of a book using your story and your friend's illustrations.

There are also ways to collaborate on the writing of a story with both partners doing the writing and the illustrations. You might start by simply brainstorming ideas and plots and characters. (See *Stories and Mini-Novels* for ideas.) Jot down possibilities as you talk so you don't forget your best ideas. As you begin to find the direction you want your story to take, one person can do the writing and both of you can contribute ideas and specific sentences. There may be a lot of crossing out and rewriting, but you can develop some good stories by working with each other's ideas as you go along. After you have written your rough copy, you can go back, reread, and make further changes before you make your final copy.

Another way of collaborating is to take turns writing different parts of the story. After you have decided on the main characters and the general direction of your story, you can decide who wants to write which parts. You may want to take turns writing every other chapter. Or one of you might want to write the beginning and the other write the ending. You can even alternate paragraph by paragraph or line by line! New characters or subplots can be added to the story as each author develops his or her own part.

The Surprise Story

The surprise story begins with no advanced planning about characters or plot. The first writer begins by setting the scene, establishing a character or two, and perhaps describing a situation or a problem. The first writer then hands the story over to the second, who decides what happens next. The story is handed back and forth with each writer adding new characters, new situations, or new problems. With this kind of story it is fun to get the characters in real tangles and then to hand the story to the other writer to untangle the problem. Stories like this may never end! But you and your partner can get together and decide on a dramatic ending.

Here are some ideas for beginnings of Surprise Stories:

- "As I finally reached the top of the jagged mountain, I couldn't believe what I saw."
- "Toby turned the ignition of his motorcycle, but instead of going forward, his cycle went straight up in the air."
- "After Sally had satisfied her curiosity about the abandoned house, she decided to leave. But the doorknob wouldn't turn."
- "I looked down the police lineup and thought I saw the man, but I couldn't be sure."
- "Jack's cat Zoe was acting very strange, like it wanted Jack to follow it."
- "Pam stood at the altar next to her fiance Paul. Suddenly, out of the corner of her eye she saw Doug appear at the back of the church."

The Circle Story

Like the surprise story, the circle story requires no advanced planning.

It requires a minimum of three authors but can involve six, ten, or even twenty lively minds adding bizarre twists and details. Each member of the writing team adds new parts to the story based on what has been written already. Begin by having one person write the first line of the story. The story is passed to the right, and the next person adds a line, and so on around the circle. The story can continue on as long as the authors are enjoying writing, with each one building on situations already developed or adding new situations, characters, and subplots.

If you have problems getting started, here are some first sentences to help you:

- "I looked down at my body. I was growing fur on my shoes, my arms, my legs—all over!"
- "Patti's parents weren't expected home for two more hours. But she could have sworn she heard the back door open . . . and then close."
- "John knew that Eric was out to get him, but he didn't think Eric would go this far."
- "Marsha felt herself shrinking, and suddenly she was looking *up* at a flower petal, instead of down at one."
- "Terry and Angela had been best friends since first grade, but now that Mark was on the scene it looked like things might change."
- "Michael had always enjoyed movies about creatures from outer space, but he didn't think they were real . . . until tonight."

The Circle Poem

The circle poem is written like the circle story, but instead of focusing on plot, character, and action, the poem emphasizes senses, feelings, and images. Here are some ideas for circle poems:

Definitions. Each person writes a line giving his/her definition of an idea or word. Possible words: *happiness, summer, cats, the sky, the wind, love, nighttime.*

Memories. Each person starts a line with "I remember" and describes a vivid memory about a past experience.

Color poems. The group selects one color, and each member writes a line of the poem with that color mentioned in the line. Alternatively, each person can write a line about a different color.

Season poems. Each person writes a line describing a season, either a season chosen in advance or about any season.

Feeling poems. The poem can be about one feeling that the group picks in advance, or there can be a mixture of feelings in the poem. Lines might begin: "I like . . ."; "I love . . ."; "I hate . . ."; "I am sad . . ."; "I am angry . . ."; "I am happy. . . ."

The Collection

You might want to work with friends to put together a whole book of stories that you have written individually. Make a book of poetry in which you and your friends include poems all on the same theme: nature poems, love poems, space poems, sports poems, superhero poems. Collaborate to make a book of limericks or a book of haiku. Collect your short stories into one volume, collaborating on table of contents, design, and illustration. (The section on *Stories and Mini-Novels* will give you ideas for stories and *A Hand-Bound Book* tells you how to bind your efforts together.)

Stories and Mini-Novels

For this project, we'll sharpen your storytelling skills and help you write a long story or a short book called a "mini-novel." For the form of your book or story, see any of the projects in the previous sections: *Scrolls; Accordian Books; Quartos; Mini-Books; A Hand-Bound Book; Collaborative Stories.* Then, instead of paper and pencil materials, we'll give you "materials" in the form of *characters* (people), *plots* (adventures), and *settings* (locations). You may also want to use some props, some objects or other things that add to the story.

Science Fiction-Fantasy

"Materials":
- *Characters*
  Space cadet
  A three-headed monster
  The mad ruler of planet Scribner
  The all-knowing space captain
  A kid your age
  His or her parents
  A robot who talks
  The glyphl
  A space "cowboy"
  General Ironfist
- *Plots*
  A runaway spaceship
  Landing on an unfamiliar planet
  Some sort of creature takes over people's minds
  The glyphl wants to go back home to Glyphylopolis
  The space kids save the day
  War with the dark forces

Peace comes to the galaxy

The sun goes out

- *Settings*

The bridge of the starship *Peatbog*

Mars

Beneath the surface of Pluto

2001 A.D.

3000 A.D.

65 B.C.

In the path of an onrushing planetoid

- *Props*

A space blaster

A robot dog

Computers that talk

Animal-like beasts that talk

Strange costumes

Mysterious languages

Space shuttles

Life-support systems

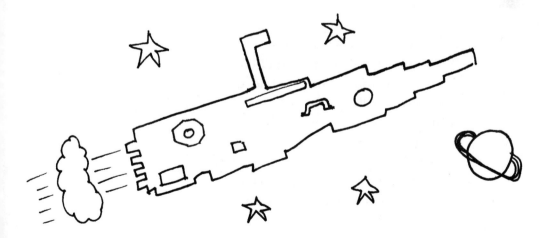

Procedures:

To write a science-fiction fantasy, let your mind loose. Choose several of the characters we have listed, or make up some outer-space critters of your own. Decide on a setting—a place where your story will happen—and a plot (or adventure). Pick an opening sentence that will interest your readers like:

- "Xerog awoke and found himself drifting through blackness."
- "'Looks harmless to me,' Sylvania thought, just before the winged rock lizard attacked her."
- "'Commander, commander! Three Terwilligan space dusters on our starboard platitude,' barked out the navigational computer."

Leave plenty of room in your book for illustrations and drawings. After you have written a draft of your story, we suggest that you read it to somebody else for comments; then make a final copy in your book.

Wild West Adventure

"Materials":
- *Characters:*

  Somebody named "Slim"

  A schoolmaster or schoolmarm

  A man so mean that dogs won't bite him

  A villain so rotten you want to throw things at him (or her)

  The local sheriff

  A friendly postmaster or storekeeper

  A coward who learns to be brave

  Somebody who keeps sheep

  Somebody who hates the sheepmen

  A funny person about ninety-two years old
- *Plots*

  Somebody held up the bank (post office, stagecoach)

The sheriff is out of town when the bad guys come
A city slicker tries to take on the tough guys
The town is going broke
The town well has gone dry
The villain turns out to have a heart of gold

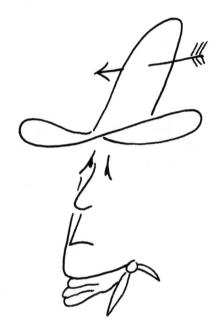

- *Settings*
  Tombstone, Arizona
  Inside a railroad train
  On the trail
  Looking for gold
  1875
  The wild west today
  In the rustlers' camp
  The town jail
- *Props*
  Boots

Saddles
A hitching post
The hardware store
Six-guns, shotguns, rifles
The sheriff's badge
Footprints
Hoofprints
The lonesome howl of a coyote

Procedures:

Westerns are filled with drama: action, conflict, and love. Start your story by describing the place where your story happens—the dusty main street of Tombstone; the crowded, rotten jail; out on the trail. Then let your hero (or villain) show up on the scene. Once that happens, just let the story flow. Don't forget the traditional ending: somebody rides off into the sunset.

Detective Thriller

"Materials":

- *Characters*
  The detective
  His or her pal at the police station
  Some kids who like to snoop around and solve things
  A handsome or beautiful but dishonest person
  Some bullies
  Innocent bystanders
  Witnesses who get confused
  Butlers, waitresses, taxi drivers who answer questions
- *Plots*
  Somebody robbed the jewelry store (bank, museum)
  Somebody kidnapped the judge's daughter (the mayor's wife, the mayor's husband, the mayor)

Somebody hijacked the train (plane, truck, boat)
Something's wrong, but nobody knows what
The detective acts like a dope, but he/she's smart
A missing person holds the main clue

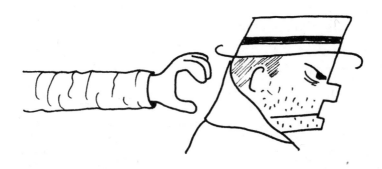

- *Settings*
  A mansion
  Downtown in a major city
  Out in the country
  In the hero's apartment
  In the police station
  In a secret hideaway
  On a ship
- *Props*
  Squeaking doors
  False clues
  Real clues
  Flashlights that don't work
  Black cats
  Fingerprints
  A tiny fleck of dust
  Yesterday's newspaper
  The telephone that rings at odd times

Procedures:

With a mystery thriller, it's important to keep your reader in suspense until the very end. Don't let us know who the criminal is. Many mystery writers like to end their stories by calling all the suspects into the room, then announcing the guilty person's name. In one famous mystery, the guilty person turns out to be the person telling the story! Be sure to throw in lots of false clues to confuse or mislead the reader.

Journals and Diaries

Most of the writing projects we have described in this book involve giving or sharing your work in some way. But some of the writing you do can be for yourself, writing that you don't necessarily want other people to read. Writers, artists, actors, dancers, politicians, doctors—all sorts of people—keep journals and diaries: records of their thoughts, feelings, ideas, and experiences. There might be several reasons you would want to keep a journal.

A writer's journal is a good place to keep track of ideas you have for poems, stories, novels, or plays. Maybe you dream up an interesting or funny character, but you don't know how to use that character in your writing. You can use your journal to write a description of the character to use later. Or perhaps you have visited an unusual place or have seen a striking event you would like to use later in a poem or story. Jot down the details in your journal. Some of what you write in your journal will go directly into your stories, some will be adapted, and some things you may never use. But you won't lose track of good possibilities if you've saved them in your journal.

You can also record your memories in a diary or journal. As you get older, you will start to forget important events or experiences from younger days. You may forget how it felt to ride a horse for the first time.

Your memories of the excitement of your first plane ride or your tenth birthday party or the sensation of the first roller coaster trip may dim. As you mature you may find it difficult to remember what it was like to be frightened or confused or sad about things that happened to you. Diaries and journals can be used to look back at experiences to review, relive, and rethink your life.

Diaries and journals are also a way of letting off steam. Often you have experiences that make you especially angry or sad, and there is no one to whom you can talk who would understand. Sometimes you just want to figure out how you feel before you try to talk to anyone about your feelings. Writing is a good way to take care of those emotions. You can write anything you want in a journal, being as angry or as hurt as you want without having to worry about how someone else will be affected. Sometimes after you have written out your feelings, you will find that they aren't as overpowering as you thought. Often you will find solutions or alternatives to problems you are dealing with. And it always helps to get if off your chest.

Though you can buy diaries with dated pages at the store, you might like to try something that gives you more space and fewer restrictions than the diary. There are various types of blank books available in stationery stores and bookstores. Some are very formal-looking black hardbound books with unlined pages. Others come in bright colors. There are also paperbound blank books that come with lined pages to make writing easier. The books come in various thicknesses and dimensions.

A better idea, and certainly less expensive, is to make your journal using the directions in *A Hand-Bound Book*. This time, however, make it with blank pages, as many as you think you might fill up in a month or a year or whatever period of time you plan to keep your journal. If you make your own journal, you can create the size, shape, and color to suit your own tastes.

Spiral notebooks or three-ring notebooks can also be adequate as a diary or a journal. Because they are inexpensive and informal, you will feel comfortable writing any old thing in them; you won't feel you have to have some earthshaking information or some profound idea before you write in your notebook.

And that's the way a journal should be. It should be a place for random thoughts, for outpourings of any sort. In choosing your journal, then, find something that you will use and enjoy writing in. We even know one person who keeps a journal that is simply a box. She writes entries for her journal whenever the spirit strikes her—on notebook paper in classes, on placemats or paper napkins in restaurants, on memo pads next to telephones. When she gets home she puts her papers in her "journal," a shoe box containing all sizes and shapes of papers written here and there in her wanderings.

Cloth-bound book

Tissue Box (Decorate)

Plain notebook

Commercial diary

Index cards (Bind together with rubber bands)

Remember, a journal or diary is kept for you. You may use it once a day, once a week, once a month, or once every six months. It is a record of what you find meaningful and worthwhile in your life. Enjoy it.

Part Three

Holiday Projects

Halloween Projects

Halloween is the first holiday of the school year and one of the most fun. Everybody enjoys getting dressed up for trick-or-treating or for parties. Halloween also offers some interesting possibilities for writing for giving. This year, consider some of the projects on the following pages.

Door Posters

Instead of buying decorations, make some of your own, including a poster or hanging for your front door that will serve as a welcome for trick-or-treaters.

Materials:
- A large piece of paper or cardboard. Use a sheet of wrapping paper or shelf paper, or several sheets of orange construction paper taped together, or a piece or two of orange poster board, or a large piece of cardboard made by cutting up a cardboard box. (The sheet can be as large as your front door.)
- Crayons, felt-tip markers, or poster paints.

Procedures:
In the center of your poster, draw a large Halloween character: a witch on a broomstick, a ghost, a black cat against a full moon, a devil, a skeleton, or a skull.

Then write a Halloween greeting across the top of the poster. Leave a space at the bottom for your friends and visitors to sign their names or to write a saying of their own.

In another variation, make your poster out of white materials in the shape of a tombstone. Have your visitors "carve" their names on the stone with a felt-tip pen.

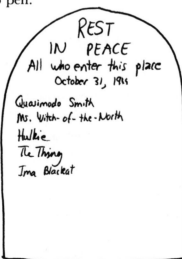

Curses, Warnings, and Epitaphs

All in the spirit of fun, create some modern-day curses, warnings, spells, or epitaphs (tombstone sayings). You can write these on full-size sheets of construction paper and hang them around the room, or you can write them on small sheets of paper the size of playing cards and give them away to trick-or-treaters or as party favors.

Materials:
- Construction paper (orange and/or white)
- Black pen
- Scissors

Procedures:
On scratch paper, write a series of curses or warnings, then recopy them on sheets of construction paper. Here are several that some of our young friends have created:

MAY CASPER THE FRIENDLY GHOST TURN UNFRIENDLY ON YOU!

I HOPE YOU GET IN TROUBLE WITH YOUR GHOUL FRIEND

MAY YOU GET NOTHING BUT HEALTH FOOD IN YOUR TRICK-OR-TREAT BAG

I HOPE THE HEADLESS HORSEMAN GETS A GOOD LOOK AT YOU!

Or make up a series of epitaphs in poetic form and copy them on sheets of paper cut to look like tombstones.

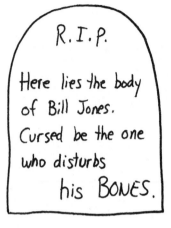

R.I.P.

Here lies the body
of Bill Jones.
Cursed be the one
who disturbs
        his BONES.

A girl named
        Sharon
lies in this grave.
When Dracula said
        "Hi"
She gave him a
        wave.

For room decorations, use a full sheet of construction paper, 9 x 12 inches or larger. You might even want to string your curses and epitaphs from the ceiling so that they turn in the air, like a mobile.

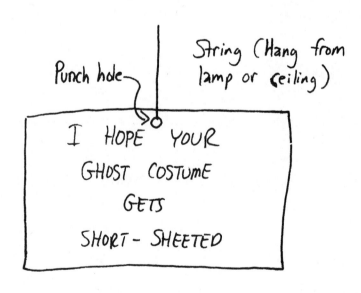

Punch hole

String (Hang from lamp or ceiling)

I HOPE YOUR
GHOST COSTUME
GETS
SHORT - SHEETED

On the other hand, you might want to give out curses, spells, or epitaphs along with candy bars this year. Cut your construction paper into squares about 2 x 3 inches and copy your lines on them. You don't need to come up with a new line for each card. Invent about five or six good ones and then copy them over until you have enough.

Ghostly Jokes

Using the same materials as for curses, you can create a set of Halloween jokes. These can be written on large sheets of paper to be used as a decoration or on small cards to be given away.

Materials:
- Construction paper (orange)
- Marking pens or crayons
- Scissors

Procedures:
Jokes can be written in a number of different styles or patterns. For example, here are several riddles written by our nine-year-old, Emily. You can put the question on one side of the card, the answer on the other.

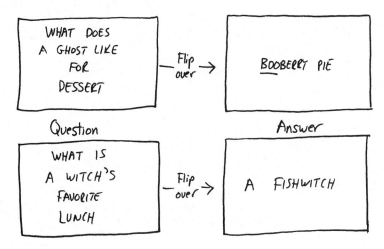

Or you can write funny sayings.

DRACULA
WAS A
NIGHT SCHOOL
DROP IN!

Here is a parody (a humorous imitation) of a well-known song written by our eleven-year-old, Steve:

"Take me out to the grave yard,
Take me out to the grave.
Buy me some blood and a dusty bone,
I don't care if I never get home.
Oh it's one, two, three bites, you're out!
At the old grave yard."

Your turn. We hope your jokes leave your friends "howling."

Eerie Tales for Late at Night

Just about everybody loves a good ghost tale. You sit in the dark listening to somebody tell a chilling story. The voice is soft until the very moment when something so horrid happens that . . . the people in the room jump for fright. Then everybody laughs and has a good time.

76

Materials:
- Just plain paper and pencil

Procedures:

You've heard ghost stories all your life so you can probably start right off writing one. Here are some special effects you might want to use:

- Clanking chains
- Squeaking door
- Abandoned house
- Mysterious phone call
- Bats
- Ancient superstitions
- Black cats
- Spider webs
- Something down in the cellar scratching
- Wind rattling the windows
- A low moan
- A high-pitched scream
- Absolute silence

And you'll need some people for your story:

- An old man or woman who looks spooky
- Somebody who says, "I'm not afraid of anything!"
- Dracula
- Frankenstein
- Witches
- Goblins
- Mummies
- Skeletons

Build up the tension in the story for as long as you can, holding the suspense until the very last moment. Then make the ending sudden . . . and terrifying.

When you've written your tale, gather up some listeners in a dark room. (Don't take the baby! We don't want to frighten the young ones.) Use a flashlight so you can read your own writing. If you want to add to the spooky effects, cover up the flashlight with red or orange cellophane.

If you are happy with the way your ghostly tale turned out, consider making it into a book with illustrations. (See *Scrolls; Accordian Books; Quartos; A Hand-Bound Book;* or *Mini-Books.*)

Thanksgiving Projects

Thanksgiving is a time when many people get together with close friends and relatives for celebration (and, of course, for eating). Our Thanksgiving projects combine both, and the arrival of guests at your door provides you with many opportunities to give the gift of writing.

Place Mats

The Thanksgiving dinner is a time when you "dress up" the table, sometimes with a centerpiece, often with the best tablecloth and fancy dishes. Add to the decorations with some hand-written, hand-decorated place mats.

Materials:
- Plain paper place mats. You can buy these at the store in packages of a dozen or two dozen. Or cut pieces of shelf paper approximately eighteen inches long.
- Felt-tip pens in several colors or colored crayons.

- Clear contact paper. (This is optional. If you want to save the mats from year to year or let people take them home, you will need to protect the mats with plastic.)

Procedures:

In the center of your place mat, copy the writing you have done. (See suggestions.) Then with felt pens or crayons, draw appropriate illustrations around the edge. Finally, if you want to preserve the place mat, cut a piece of clear contact paper just the size of the mat, peel off the backing paper, and carefully place over the design.

Plain paper place mat

Write your poem or story

Add illustrations

To protect the mat, cover it with clear contact paper → Clear contact

Decorated mat

Writing ideas for your place mats include the following:

Welcome messages. Write the name of the guest toward the top of the mat and then draft a simple welcome message. Make it clear why you are happy that the person is joining you for the holiday.

Original poetry. Write one or several poems for the occasion. You might pen something about the autumn, about the Thanksgiving spirit, or about the person who will be visiting you. One good way to write is to begin each line of the poem with the phrase, "Thanksgiving is _____," and then fill in the blanks.

Thanksgiving recipes. Write some of the recipes that are Thanksgiving favorites on the mat, then illustrate. (See the next project, *Holiday Cookbook,* for more ideas.)

Original Thanksgiving stories. Every holiday has its stories and myths and superstitions. Why not create some new ones for Thanksgiving and write them on your place mats? Some titles for Thanksgiving tales include:

- How the Turkey Got Its Gobble
- Where Pumpkin Pie Came From
- The *Last* Thanksgiving Dinner
- How the Turkey Got Its Stuffing
- Why the Sweet Potato Is Sweet

NOTE: This project is not one that must be limited to Thanksgiving. You could make place mats for any holiday or special occasion. They're especially attractive for birthdays.

Holiday Cookbook

Since much of the Thanksgiving celebration centers around the kitchen, consider writing a cookbook for the occasion.

Materials:
- Use any of the types of book described in Part II: *Accordian Books; Scrolls; Quartos,* etc. Pick a kind that you especially like to do.
  or
- Make multiple copies of your book by photocopying or mimeographing. (Instructions follow.)

Procedures:

This project will involve a little bit of research and, very possibly, some delightful time spent hanging around the kitchen.

If your mom and/or dad are doing all the cooking, ask them to tell you the recipes as they prepare the dinner. In a notebook, put each recipe on a separate page—one for the turkey, one for the dessert, one for the vegetables, and so on. Then copy the recipes into your book, which you can prepare beforehand.

Sometimes holiday guests will bring food, too. If that's the case, you might want to interview each guest/cook to find out how the dish was prepared. Again, copy the recipes in your book.

After the dinner, while everybody is relaxing, watching football on TV, or just moaning and groaning about how much he or she ate, you might work on your book, copying recipes, adding illustrations, etc.

If you don't have too many guests, you might want to make a copy for each one. But if a lot of people came, then copying by hand might be too time-consuming, and you might want to arrange to have your book copied by one of the following methods:

Mimeograph. Most schools and churches have mimeograph machines that make printed copies. Check around places where you are a member or a student to see if you can get your cookbook printed as a special favor. If you are successful, somebody will have to make a stencil for you by typing the recipes on a wax sheet that goes into the machine. A secretary or the person who typed your stencil will need to run copies for you. After the printing is done, you can add color illustrations and bind the book.

Photocopying. This is the familiar Xerox process by which you put a piece of paper into a machine and get multiple copies out the other side. No stencil is needed. Simply take the final copy of your book to a copying center and get as many copies as you need, at a cost of five to ten cents per page. As with mimeograph, you may want to add color illustrations to personalize your book before you give it away.

The Historical Thanksgiving

Many legends have grown about the Indians, the Pilgrims, and the first Thanksgiving day. In this project, you will read up on Thanksgiving and then write the true story as you understand it.

Materials:

- Use any of the books described in Part II: *Hand-Bound Books, Mini-Books,* etc.

Procedures:

Go to your school or city library and check out some books about Thanksgiving. If you know how to use the card catalog, you can look under the headings of Thanksgiving or Pilgrims. Ask the librarian to help you find a book or two that tells the accurate story of the Pilgrims' arrival in New England, their first year here, and the first Thanksgiving. Then read and enjoy the books. (Talk about them to other people, too. You'll be a real expert on this holiday.)

After you've read carefully, retell the story in your own words, and write it down in your book. You might want to tell it as a simple story, beginning at the beginning and writing to the end, but it might be fun to try one of these possibilities:

- Pretend you are in a time machine that carries you back to the first Thanksgiving. Describe the scene that you see.
- Be an on-the-scene reporter and interview some of the people there. Interview some of the Pilgrims, for example, and try to put their feelings into words:

You: This has been a long, hard year for you. How do you feel now?

Pilgrim: We are grateful to be alive and to have this harvest. That is why we are giving thanks today.

- Write a short play that shows what happened on that first Thanksgiving. (If you do it this way, show your teacher. He or she may want you to have your play acted by fellow students.)

- Pretend you are a television producer planning a "special" on the first Thanksgiving. Write a description of what you would like the TV program to be about.
- Become a Pilgrim or an Indian. Write about Thanksgiving as if you were one of the people who was actually there. What do you think? What do you feel? How does the food taste? How did you prepare it? What do you say to your family and friends on this special occasion?
- Pretend you are a Pilgrim magically transported to the twentieth century on Thanksgiving day. What do you think about the way we Americans celebrate it? What else do you see that amazes you? For what do you think Americans should give thanks? How does their life in modern America differ from yours over 300 years ago?

Whichever way of writing the story you choose, illustrate your book to make it attractive as well as informative.

Family Stories

At Thanksgiving time (or at any time when many members of your family get together), collect stories and memoirs which people have to share. Get them down in a book so that they won't be forgotten.

Materials:
- Writing paper and pens and pencils for your family and guests.

Procedures:
Explain to your guests that you want to make a collection of their favorite stories about themselves. (Stories like these are called "memoirs.") At an appropriate time of the day, perhaps while everybody is relaxing after dinner, pass out sheets of paper and ask them to write for you. Read off a list of topics that they might enjoy writing about:

- A time I got in trouble as a child.
- Memories of another Thanksgiving.
- Memories of my parents.
- Memories of my own children when they were young.
- Where I went to school and some of my teachers.
- My room at home, years ago.
- My first trip away from home.
- My first job.
- The most unforgettable character I ever met.
- Strange and unusual happenings in my life.

If people are having trouble writing, suggest that they just write their stories as letters to you. When everybody has finished writing, ask each person to read his or her story aloud to the group. Keep a sheet of paper handy yourself, for it is likely that as people relax, they will tell many more stories about themselves. Like a good reporter, you can jot down what they say and write it up later.

Then collect all your guests' writing, add any stories that you copied down, and make it into a book. (See *A Hand-Bound Book.*) As another possibility, you simply might want to punch holes in the pages and place them in a looseleaf notebook so that you can add more stories later. Make it a family tradition that each year, every person adds a story to your growing collection of memoirs.

Christmas and Chanukah Projects

Christmas and Chanukah are known as the seasons for giving. Few gifts are appreciated as much as those made by the gift giver. We hope that some of the following projects will suggest ways that you can give of yourself during this season.

Printed Holiday Cards

During the holiday season, Christmas, Chanukah, and New Year's cards flood the mails and our homes. The pleasure in sending and receiving cards is much greater when we receive one expressed in the words and sentiments of the sender, rather than a preprinted card with a standard message. Making your own greeting cards is no more expensive than buying them, but the card will be much more valued than the store-bought varieties. You might want to make a few cards by hand for the most important people in your life, but for multiple copies, offset printing (described in *Making Your Own Stationery*) offers a relatively inexpensive way of making many cards—100 or more.

Materials:
- White paper—8½ x 11
- Black pen, paint, felt-tip marker
- Blue pencil

Procedures:
One type of offset printed card involves printing on only one side to make a folded card. Divide your 8½ x 11 inch sheet of paper into four equal sections. Your completed page layout will look like this:

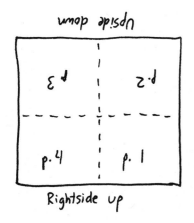

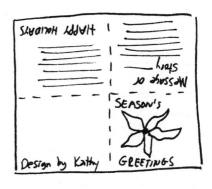

85

Another layout allows you to make two different kinds of cards from an 8½ x 11 inch sheet of paper cut in half after it is printed. For this card, you need to have both sides printed. In order to do that, you draw and write on two 8½ x 11 inch sheets of paper. One sheet will be for pages one and four of your cards; the other sheet will make up pages two and three of the cards.

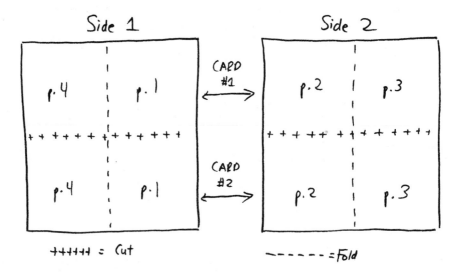

Before deciding on the design and contents of your printed card, try out several possibilities. For the message, you might like to write a short wish or greeting expressing your hopes and feelings for the friends to whom you are sending the card. You might like to write out a list of wishes and hopes for people. Think of new ways of stating old sentiments and then choose the best one to go on your card. You might like to write a poem describing your feelings about the holiday. You could write a narrative about your family and their activities of the year, or you might write a fictional story or parable about the holiday. The next three sections provide more ideas that can be used in holiday greetings.

Experiment with pictures and designs for your cards too. *Making Your Own Stationery* describes potato print techniques that you can use. Make your own version of traditional holiday designs and symbols—

wreaths, Christmas trees, Santa, snowflakes, sleighs, menorahs, etc.

After you have sketched out your greeting card, carefully put the design on your layout sheets. Use light blue pencil to outline your pictures and text. Then write the words and draw the design with black pen. Remember that everything—printing and design—must be done in black so that it will show up when it is printed.

Paper for printing your cards comes in various colors and in different paper weights. The printer will show you samples of the kinds of paper you can use. Light paper is probably better for cards that are folded. Heavier and somewhat more expensive paper is better for cards that have only a single fold.

To make envelopes for your cards, purchase blank sheets of paper—the same number as the number of cards you are sending. Fold your paper around the card, following the figure.

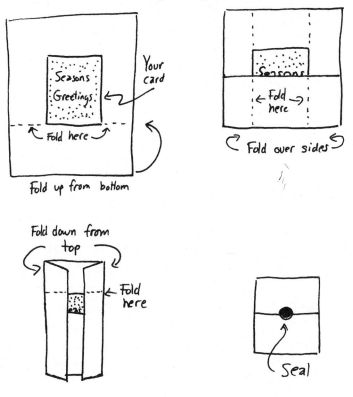

Seal the open edge with sealing wax, which is available at stationery stores, or use sticky holiday seals or brightly colored packaging tape.

Chanukah Traditions Book

Several kinds of Chanukah traditions books make excellent gifts for family or for friends during the holiday season. You might retell stories of heroism surrounding the origin of Chanukah; you might describe some of the traditions your family observes during the holiday; or you might like to write a book of memories of past Chanukahs. See the book projects in Part II, then write a Chanukah traditions book using some of the suggestions that follow:

The History of Chanukah. In retelling the history of Chanukah, consider including some of the following stories:

- The invasion of Antiochus's soldiers into Modin and the reaction of Mattathias and his sons.
- Judah Maccabee's victory at Emmaus.
- The return of the Maccabees to Jerusalem.
- The miracle of the oil.
- The story of Hannah and her seven sons who refused to bow to Zeus.
- The origin of the dreidel.
- The story of Judith and the origin of latkes.

Family Celebrations During Chanukah. Some of your celebrations or family traditions are so much a part of your life that you don't notice them. Take a closer look at your holiday, and write a series of descriptions about your special way of observing Chanukah.

Do you have a menorah that has special significance to your family? Has it been handed down for generations? Or was it made by someone in your family? Who lights the menorah? Do you put it in a special place after it's lit? The same place every night? Do you have a family ceremony surrounding the lighting of the candles? What blessings do you say?

Do people in your family prepare special food for Chanukah? Do you have latkes during Chanukah? When? Include a favorite family recipe for latkes or other special foods you like to have during the holidays in your book.

What are your gift-giving traditions during the holiday? Do you get a gift every day? When?

Do you have special story times or games during Chanukah? Do you play spin the dreidel? Do you have a special dreidel for the occasion? What prizes do you use?

Does your family gather at someone's house during Chanukah? Where do you gather? Who is there?

Memories of Chanukahs Past. Parents and grandparents will appreciate a book that describes your memories of Chanukah. Perhaps some of your memories have begun to fade. Try writing down everything you can remember on paper. Write down every happy, exciting, or even sad event or experience you can remember from other celebrations. The more you write the more you will begin to remember. After you have gathered your random ideas, sort them into a narrative or a series of little stories.

After you have written your story, make it into a book. Illustrate your book with drawings, paintings, or add photography that your family has saved from previous Chanukah celebrations.

The Christmas Story

Though the Christmas story is old and has been told many times, your own version can make it special—for you and for those with whom you share the story. One way of recreating the Christmas story is to tell it through the eyes and words of someone else. How did the following experience the events of the first Christmas? What did they see and feel of the events surrounding Christmas? Write the story as one of the following characters might have told it:

- Mary
- Joseph
- Jesus
- The donkey
- A wise man
- A shepherd
- An animal at the manger
- A child staying at the inn
- An angel
- The innkeeper

You might like to try writing the "perfect" Christmas story. Go back to the Biblical versions of the story found in the Gospels and gather all of the information they provide about the events leading up to the birth of Jesus. Use that information and eliminate the myths and stories added by other authors' recreations. Piece the story together using only what you find in the Bible.

Another project is to retell parts of the Christmas story through poetry. Poems usually focus on pictures rather than on stories; thus they only describe a small part of a scene, rather than trying to take in everything. (Remember: Poetry does not *have* to rhyme.) Some of the following scenes might offer good possibilities for creating vivid pictures of the first Christmas:

- The appearance of the angels.
- The looks on the faces of the shepherds when they first see the angels or Jesus.
- Mary holding Jesus.
- The finery of the wise men compared with the roughness of the manger.
- The baby's reactions to the events of his first night.
- A picture of the manger.

Some writers have used the Biblical accounts of the Christmas story to create new versions, stories like *The Little Drummer Boy, The Littlest Angel,* and *Amahl and the Night Visitors.* The events of the first Christmas have inspired the creation of stories for people of all ages. Why not invent a new version of the Christmas story? You might describe it as if *you* were there, a visitor in Bethlehem that night. Alternatively, you might write about it from the point of view of someone your age who found and prepared the manger for Mary and Joseph and their baby.

There are several ways you can give a gift of the Christmas story, including the books described in Part II: *Making Your Own Books.* Perhaps better, "give" your writing by reading it aloud as a part of a family gathering on Christmas Eve or Christmas Day.

Original Holiday Tales

Christmas, Chanukah, and New Year's tales can be about any characters, events, or settings you can imagine—science fiction, comedy, fantasy, mystery, adventure. Stories can be based on your own experiences or spring from your wildest fantasies. They can be written for adults, for kids your age, or for younger children. They can be given as gifts in the form of books or shared through reading aloud. The following is a list of titles that can be used for holiday tales, but we suspect you may want to create titles for tales of your own.

- Christmas on Mars
- Santa's Nightmare
- New Year's in Orbit
- The House Santa Forgot
- The Case of the Missing Menorah
- The Broken New Year's Resolution
- The Return of the Christmas Star
- A New Year's Party (That Ended Too Late)
- The Elves' Christmas Party

For these holiday tales, make a cover or binding using holiday wrapping paper.

Materials:

- Wrapping paper
- Regular writing paper
- Ribbon or yarn
- Scissors
- Glue

Procedures:

When you have completed your story, stack up all the pages. Cut two pieces of brightly colored wrapping paper just a little larger than those sheets to serve as a cover. Punch two holes through both the cover and the story and bind them together with ribbon or yarn, and tie a big bow.

Then cut out a small piece of paper. Write on the title of your story, and paste that to the front cover as shown.

Punch cover and pages. Tie with ribbon or yarn.

Add title.

Add holiday decorations.

In addition, you might want to embellish your cover, adding fancy bows, holly sprigs, bells, or other holiday decorations.

Valentine's Day Projects

Saint Valentine's Day is one of the nicer holidays of the year. It comes in the middle of winter when the weather is bleak, and the bright colors associated with the day help to cheer everyone up. You don't have to give a lot of expensive gifts on Valentine's Day, and just about everybody enjoys giving and receiving cards. Of course you can buy cards, ready-made, but it is a lot more fun for you and meaningful for others if you make your own. We have already shown you in the project called *Greeting Cards* how to make some kinds of cards. You can probably figure out how to adapt those projects to Valentine's Day quite easily. Just stock up on red and white construction paper, some ribbon, and some "lace." (Buy frilly paper doilies at the paper products section of the stationery store or the supermarket.) Then let your imagination go to produce a handsome collection of cards: large ones, small ones, heart-shaped ones, square ones, cards that say "I love you," cards that say, "I'm glad you're my friend," and so on.

The other Valentine's Day projects that we suggest will help you create some cards and gifts that are unusual, starting with:

The World's Largest Valentine Card

Materials:

- Find a cardboard box—the larger the better. The best place to look is at an appliance store. Ask for a discarded refrigerator box. If you can't find one, an old television box would be all right. In short, get the largest piece of cardboard you can lay your hands on.
  or
- Buy a large sheet of red poster board at a stationery store. If you choose this option; you won't need the red paint mentioned in the next item.
- Red paint—get *either* a spray can of red paint or a regular can of bright red "glossy" paint.

93

- White paint—you'll need a small can, about ½ pint at the most.
- Paint brushes—a small artist's brush for lettering and a larger one if you're not using spray paint.
- White construction or shelf paper.
- Scissors or sharp knife (use only with supervision).

Procedures:

First cut up your cardboard box to make a large flat sheet of cardboard. This may be a tough job, so get an adult to help you. You can leave the cardboard rectangular or, if you'd like, cut it into a heart shape. Use a knife for cutting heavy cardboard; a scissors will do for poster board.

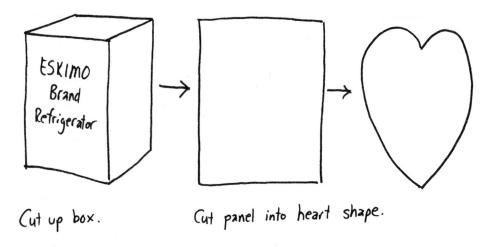

Cut up box.   Cut panel into heart shape.

Paint the cardboard red on one side, using spray paint or a brush and a can of paint. (Of course, if you're using red poster board, you can skip this part.) It may take several coats of paint to get your Valentine bright red and shiny. (Suggestion 1: If your box has printing on it, paint the *other* side. That way you won't have to waste a lot of paint trying to cover up the letters. Suggestion 2: Do this in a basement or a garage. Put down lots of newspapers before you begin.)

While the paint is drying, figure out what you want to say on your card. This is a special Valentine, so you'll want to give it to someone, or to several people, who are special. You might give it to your parents, to your whole family, to that certain special someone. (Let's hope that someone doesn't live too far away. Your Valentine will be a tough one to deliver.)

Then write your message in white paint on your card. Add appropriate Valentine's Day symbols—a cupid, hearts, etc. If you wish to add a

fringed border, cut it out of pieces of construction paper or shelf paper, and after sculpting out a design, glue the border to the back of the card.

"Sculpt" pieces of paper

WHO LOVES YOU THE MOST?

Glue on back of card to create "fringe"

The World's Largest Valentine is a card your Valentine will not soon forget.

Valentine Graffiti Wall

Graffiti are slogans or sayings that people write on walls in public places. No, we're not suggesting that you send your Valentine's Day greetings by defacing public property. This project is a more civilized variation where you and your friends send Valentine's wishes on a large sheet of paper or cardboard that is fastened to a wall. This is a good project to do with your class at school or with a group of friends at a party.

Materials:
- Large sheet of paper (shelf paper or butcher paper) or piece of cardboard (The leftovers from the *World's Largest Valentine* might do.)
- Felt-tip pens, crayons, pens, or pencils

Procedures:
Fasten your paper or cardboard to the wall and give everybody pens, pencils, or crayons. The object is for each person in the group to write a message to every other person. You can send Valentine's greetings, friendship messages, or any other kind of note that is appropriate. Everybody crowds around the graffiti wall and writes. (If your group is a big one, it might be good to post a list with everybody's name on it. That way it is easier to remember to send messages to everybody.) Afterward, you

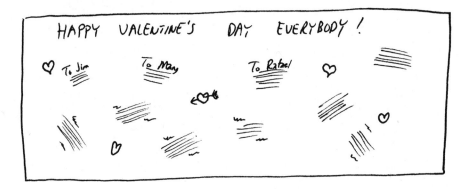

spend time at the wall looking for all the messages that were sent to you personally. As a final touch, members of the group might want to add Valentine's decorations and symbols in the few blank spaces that remain.

Valentine Photograph-Autograph Album

This might be called a writing-for-sharing project because you get to keep what you have made. Since Valentine's Day is a time for renewing friendships, why not make a collection of your friends' photographs and autographs? (Note: This is another good project for your school class or circle or friends to do. That way everybody gets a book in the end.)

Materials:
- Sheets of construction paper, 9 x 12 inches or larger
- Photo-mounting corners (Ask for a packet of these at a photo store. They are inexpensive.)
- Ribbon or yarn for bookbinding
- Pen and ink

Procedures:
First prepare some pages for your book. Select the colors of paper that you like best and turn them the wide way. You can punch holes for binding along the left edge of each page.

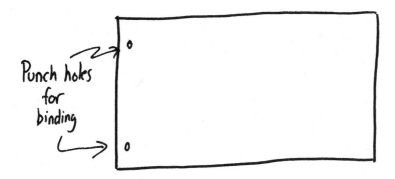

Next collect photographs and autographs from your friends. Ask each friend to let you have a picture. Often you will all have school photos or you may have snapshots to share. (Nobody should have to go out to spend a lot of money to get a picture taken.) When a friend gives you a picture, carefully mount it on one of your pages. Then have the friend write you a short note and sign his or her autograph. (While a friend is signing your book, you can be signing his or hers.)

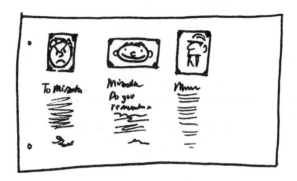

When you have completed your collection, stack up the pages, add one at the front and the back for covers, and string them together with ribbon or yarn. Write a title on the cover and indicate that this is your Valentine's Day Photo Album for 19??.

Bind
with
String
or
yarn

A VALENTINE'S DAY
Photo/Autograph Album

Collected by
        Miranda Trueheart

February 14, 19XX

A Valentine Book

We often think of books as being square or rectangular, but there's no reason why they have to be. Why not make a book shaped like a heart to give to a friend on Valentine's Day?

Materials:
- Red and white construction paper, 9 x 12 inches or larger
- Staples or ribbon or yarn for binding
- Scissors

Procedures:

On a single sheet of construction paper, red or white, draw a freehand heart shape. Go as close to the edges as you can. Go all the way to the edge for about three inches on the left side. This will give you a flat spot that is useful in binding.

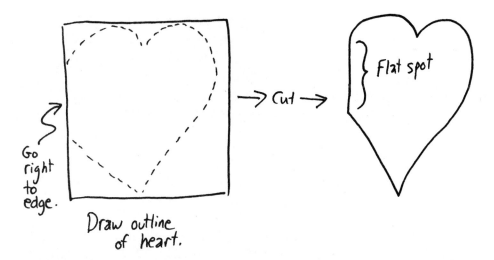

Now cut more pages to exactly the same shape and stack them up to make a book. Staple along the left edge to bind the pages together or punch two holes and tie up the pages with ribbon or yarn.

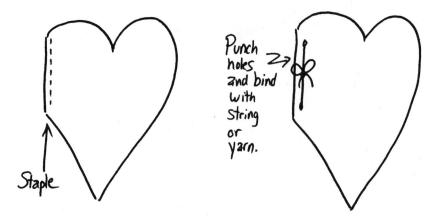

That gives you an empty book. Now what? Here are some ideas for writing on the theme of Valentine's Day:

Love stories. Create some stories of romance. Boy meets girl. Boy falls in love. Girl won't have him. Tears. Getting back together. Happy ending. (If you ever watch soap operas on television, you might write your own "soap.")

Cupid's tricks. Cupid is forever shooting his arrows at people, causing them to fall in love. Many stories and plays have been written about this theme. You write one, showing what happens when Cupid's arrow strikes an unsuspecting boy or girl, man or woman.

Valentine poetry. If you like to write poems, copy your best into a Valentine's book to give to someone special.

Springtime Writing Projects

In the spring a young person's fancy lightly turns to thoughts of love. Or perhaps to thoughts of frogs, allergies, and getting out of school. In any case, springtime presents many opportunities for you to put pen to paper to come up with some attractive, readable writing projects.

Religious Murals

Both Easter and Passover are based on vivid, important historical events. Create a mural depicting the significant events surrounding the holiday you celebrate.

Materials:
- White shelf paper, butcher paper, or paper from the end of a newspaper roll (available through newspaper offices)
- Paint, crayons, or felt-tip pens

Procedures:

Divide the length of your paper into panels, making one picture for each panel. Draw pictures to represent some of the important events of the holiday. For example:

Easter: The Last Supper; Jesus in Gethsemene; Judas's kiss and betrayal; Jesus before Pontius Pilate; Jesus on the cross; Jesus risen from the dead.

Passover: Joseph interpreting Pharaoh's dream; Joseph reunited with his family; Moses on the Nile; the ten plagues; the crossing of the Red Sea; the baking of the matzo.

Under each picture, describe what is happening and the significance of each event in the religious celebration.

Divide paper into "panels"

The events that you depict on your mural also make good subjects for poetry. Focus on the details of a small event, rather than trying to tell the whole story in one poem. If you want to tell the whole story, write a series of poems, each using vivid details—pictures, colors, action—so that the reader of the poem feels he or she is there. Add your poems to the mural, either directly under the pictures they illustrate or surrounding the mural.

Find a wall to display the mural so that guests can examine it.

Note: In a variation of this project, you might want to do an Easter Bunny Mural. Make up a tale about the rabbit and illustrate it on the panels of your mural. Then write the story beneath.

Writing on Eggshells

Many cultures and countries have the tradition of decorating eggs at Easter time. Sometimes when the eggs are made from porcelain, quartz, painted paper mache, glass, gold, silver, or china, they become valuable works of art. This project shows you how to create beautiful gifts using the real thing—hen's eggs.

DECORATED HOLLOW EGGS
Materials:
- Fresh eggs
- Straight pin
- Fine point felt-tip pens—get permanent markers, not the ones labeled "nonsoluble" or "washable." Get pens in many different colors.

Procedures:
Begin by hollowing out the number of eggs that you want to make into gifts. (Better make one or two extras for practice and in case of accidents.) Take your straight pin—a long hat pin works best—and poke a tiny hole in each end of the egg, being careful not to crack the egg. Move

the pin gently around in the hole, gradually widening it to be larger—but not much larger—than a pin prick. Place your lips over the hole at one end and gently blow, forcing the insides of the egg out the other hole into a bowl. (Save those eggs in the bowl; they can be used for cakes, scrambled eggs, or omelettes.)

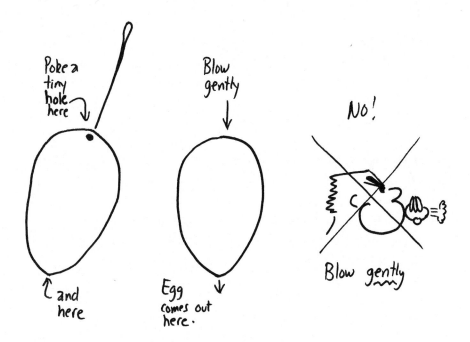

When the egg is hollow, write your message and your designs on the outside with felt-tip pen. Hold the egg gently with your thumb and middle finger, being careful not to crush it by pressing too hard.

Messages for your egg might describe spring, rabbits and chicks, new life, flowers, sunshine, and spring showers. These could be written as short poems. Or you might want to create sayings for your eggs: "Spring is . . ." or "Easter is . . ." You could even tell a mini-tale, writing a spiral around the egg. You can create special eggs for your friends, with their names and something about them. Or, write a continued story that has separate chapters on eggs numbered 1, 2, 3, etc.

After your writing is done, create colorful designs and pictures and present your gift with the message: *Fragile!*

DYED EGGS

Materials:

- Eggs—hard-boiled.
- Dye—a commercial Easter egg dye kit, or food coloring. Check the package for instructions on how to make Easter egg dye.
- Felt-tip pens—permanent, not water soluble.
- White or yellow crayons.

Procedures:

You can write on eggs before you dye them, using the writing ideas suggested in the previous section.

Procedure 1: Write on the eggs with dark—preferably black—felt-tip pen. Then prepare batches of dye according to the instructions on the package. Dip your egg in the dye, and the writing will show through. (Be careful not to dye your egg too dark or the writing will not show up. It's best to stick to light colors—pinks and yellows—rather than the darker blues and purples.

Procedure 2: Write your message before you dye the eggs, using white or yellow crayon. This is a bit tricky, because it is difficult to see where you have written, but if you hold the egg up to the light just right, you will be able to see the letters. The wax forms a "resist," where the dye won't stick. When you dye your eggs, the places you have written will remain white or eggshell color. This time it will be better to use dark colors for contrast when you dye; pinks and yellows don't work so well.

Organize an Easter Egg hunt. No matter what your friends' religion, almost everybody enjoys scurrying around looking for eggs. If the eggs have special messages, the event will be that much more fun.

May Baskets

In ancient Rome, the first day of May was celebrated with gifts of blossoms presented to Flora, the goddess of flowers. Since then, people in different countries have celebrated May Day by gathering flowers, dancing, singing, and holding processions. In parts of this country, the Maypole dance and May baskets are part of the celebration. The May basket is filled with spring flowers and left secretly at a friend's door front. A spring story or poem can also be tucked into the May basket.

Materials:
- A two-pound plastic margarine container
- Ribbon or yarn
- Crepe paper—three different springtime colors, perhaps yellow, pink, and light blue or green
- Flour and water paste
- Scissors
- Fresh flowers

Procedures:
Begin by making the May basket. Cut each of three colors of crepe paper into strips one inch wide, using the entire length of the crepe

paper. Tie the three ends together and fasten them to the arm of a chair. Braid the three strands together. (If you don't know how to braid, ask someone who does. It's easy to learn.)

Next, wrap the braid around the margarine container and glue it in place as follows:

1. Make glue from one cup of flour, mixed with enough water to make it about the consistency of ketchup.
2. Dip about six to eight inches of the braid into the paste at one time. Wipe off the excess.
3. Wind the braid around the margarine container, which you place upside down on the table. (Put it on some newspapers.)
4. Start the braid in the center of the bottom of the container. Make a tiny circle in the middle and continue winding each circle larger and larger until none of the container shows.

If you run out of braid, stop and make another one, using more strips of crepe paper.

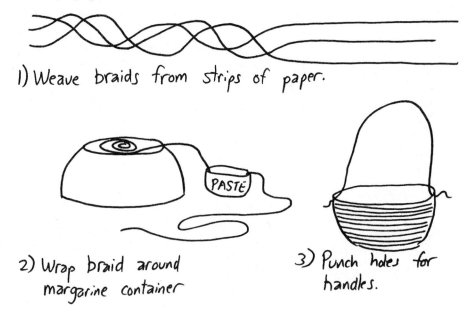

1) Weave braids from strips of paper.

2) Wrap braid around margarine container

3) Punch holes for handles.

106

After you have covered the entire container, allow twenty-four hours for it to dry. Then poke two holes near the top of the basket, directly across from one another. String yarn, ribbon, or another piece of crepe paper braid through the holes to make a handle for the basket.

Just before you are ready to deliver your basket, place your bouquet of flowers and your message in it. The message should be bright and hopeful, colorful and fanciful. Write poems and stories, letting your imagination go wild. Write about:

- Flora, the goddess of flowers.
- Elves and fairies in hidden forests.
- The animal kingdom and its spring celebrations.
- The secrets of the flowers.
- Newborn animals.

You might enjoy doing a springtime acrostics poem. Write a word related to spring vertically on a sheet of paper. Then use each letter of that word as the beginning of a line in your poem.

Write your message on a pretty piece of paper, perhaps one you have

During Spring
All the flowers show their
Faces, bringing
Fun to cloudy places.
One of the best is the
Daffodil.
I
Love it
So much

107

decorated yourself. (See *Making Your Own Stationery.*) Tuck the message in with some spring flowers and deliver your basket to your friend's door early in the morning of May 1.

Spring Nature Journal

If you love nature and the out-of-doors, spring can be the best season of all. Nature seems to change by the minute during spring, with plants poking out of the ground, buds appearing on trees, and bushes and flowers bursting into bloom overnight. If you were bored with being indoors all winter, you might like to spend some time exploring outside, discovering the progress spring makes in your part of the country and in your neighborhood. Even if you live in the city you can find a park or zoo to study. Keep track of your discoveries in a nature diary or journal.

See *Journals and Diaries* for ideas about a book in which to keep your ideas. You can make a book yourself, or buy a notebook to use. Some ideas for writing:

Animals. What changes do you see in wildlife as the season progresses? Do new birds appear? How do the activities of the little animals—squirrels, moles, rabbits, chipmunks—change as the season progresses? Have you seen any new babies among the birds or animals? When do they come out? Can you discover where they live?

Trees and Bushes. What changes do the trees and bushes in your area go through? What leaves or blossoms do you see first? How long do the blossoms last? What follows the blossoms?

Flowers. What flowers come out of the ground first? How long do they last? Which flowers bloom and last and which come and die? Does your family plant flowers in the spring? How long does it take the plants to grow? Keep track of their progress during the season.

Creative Writing. Consider doing some creative writing about what you see. Write your observations as poems, concentrating on your sensations to communicate a real feeling for nature in spring. Describe what you see, smell, hear, taste, feel.

Haiku is a Japanese poetry form that concentrates on describing pictures in nature in a very short space. The first line is five syllables, the second is seven, the last is five. (Don't feel you have to stick exactly to that form; if you have something good to say, you can use more or fewer syllables.) One example:

> Hungry babies peep
> Tiny birds, huge beaks stretch wide
> To take the fat worm.

Nature Samples. In addition to descriptions of your neighborhood, you might like to include actual samples—small pressed flowers, molted feathers, the first leaves from the maple, a flowered twig from the cherry tree.

Or take photographs of spring to accompany your descriptions. You might even want to make paintings or drawings of the progress of spring.

After you have completed your journal, you might like to share your findings with a pen pal, friend, or cousin who lives in another section of the country. Alternatively, you might send it to grandparents who live far away.

Now think about charting the progress of summer!

Index

Books: accordian, 40; animated, 48; Chanukah traditions, 88; for children, 53; collaborative, 56; folded, 46; hand-bound, 49; holiday cookbook, 80; mini-books, 47; quartos, 42; signature, 45; unfolding, 43; Valentine, 99

Calligraphy, 8
Cards: birthday, 24; get well, 25; greeting, 21; holiday, 85; letter-cards, 13; secret-friend, 28; world's largest Valentine, 93 (*see also* postcards)
Chanukah, projects for, 84; holiday cards, 85; holiday tales, 91; traditions book, 88
Christmas, projects for, 84; holiday cards, 85; holiday tales, 91; story retold, 89
Collections of writing, 59
Cookbook, holiday, 80

Detective thriller stories, 64
Diaries, 66

Eggshells, writing on, 102

Family stories, 83
Family tree, 18
Fortune cookies, 30

Halloween, projects for, 71; curses, 73; door posters, 71; eerie tales, 76; epitaphs, 73; ghostly jokes, 75; warnings, 73
Holiday projects (*see* Chanukah, Christmas, Halloween, Springtime, Thanksgiving, Valentine's Day)